Man dedicates life to peace

Spreads pacifism nationwide

By CHRIS LOGAN
Colorado Daily Staff Writer

For five years, he has traveled the countrys_ ___king to those he meets along the_ ___violence, the need to re_ ___ other, and the p_ ___ld for the

He c__
he adopted afte_
dropped the name he h_
and set out on ___

the Peace Pil_
was killed in a car ac_

Peace Pilgrim Says Fear Biggest Barrier to Love

'Peace' spreading the word

By GREG GERSO_
Staff Writer

He goes by th_ ___
grim II, but ma_
"Peace."

Peace doesn't li_ to talk much about his past, like giving his real name, or what he did before decid-

___grown
_British accent,
_is mission is to help
__work toward peace by getting people to first find their inner peace.

"I'm trying to bring people to the realization that we've talked about peace for thousands of years and

Peace pays visit to torn community

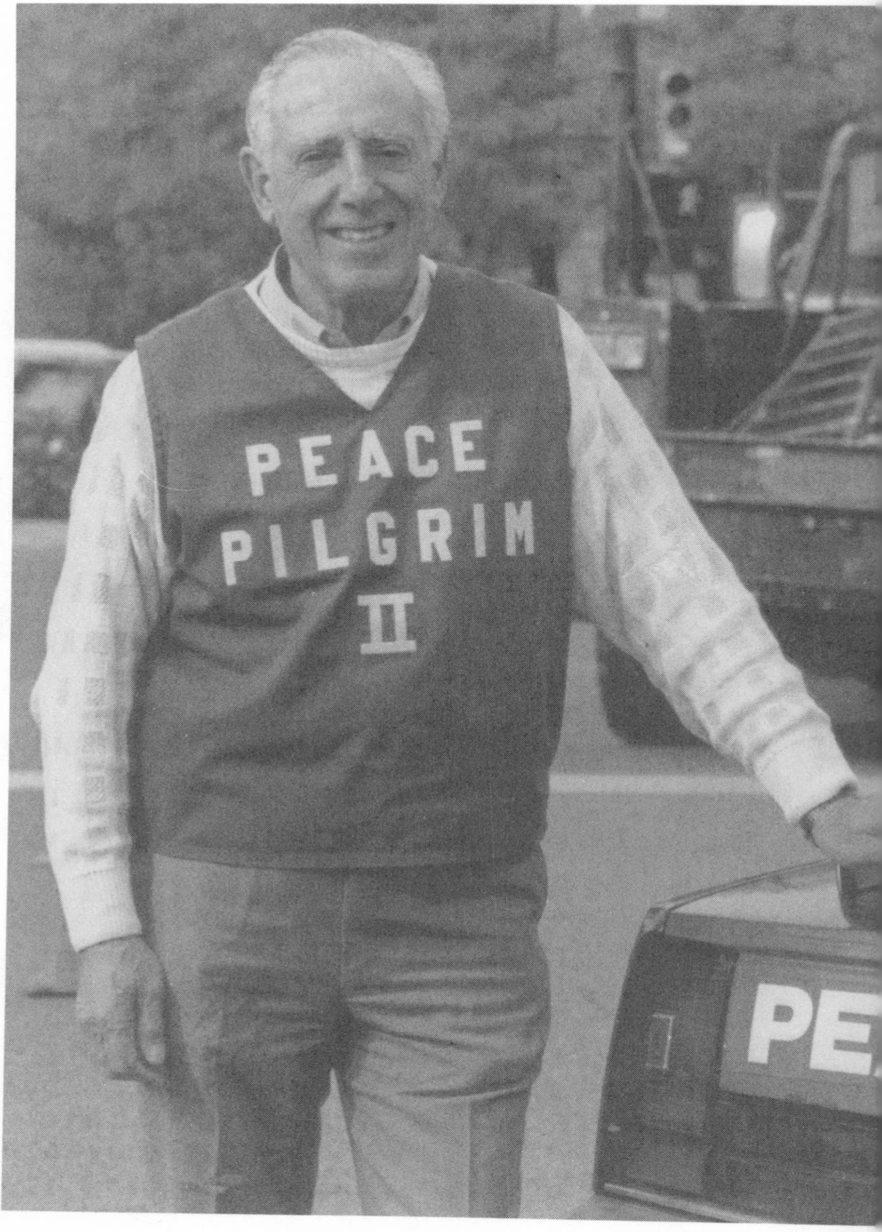
PEACE
PILGRIM
II

Enjoying the Journey

THE ADVENTURES, TRAVELS, AND TEACHINGS OF PEACE PILGRIM II

PEACE PILGRIM II

Blue Dolphin
1995

Published by Blue Dolphin Publishing, Inc.
P.O. Box 1920, Nevada City, CA 95959
Orders: 1-800-643-0765

ISBN: 0-931892-94-5

Library of Congress Cataloging in Publication Data

Peace Pilgrim II, 1926–
    Enjoying the journey : the adventures, travels, and teachings
of Peace Pilgim II / Peace Pilgrim II.
        p.   cm.
    ISBN 0-931892-94-5 : $10.00
    1. Conduct of life. 2. Peace of mind. 3. Spiritual life.
4. Peace Pilgrim II, 1926– . I. Title.
BJ1581.2.P376   1994
170'.44—dc20   94-36788
                                                        CIP

Printed in the United States of America by
Blue Dolphin Press, Inc., Grass Valley, California

10   9   8   7   6   5   4   3   2   1

This book is dedicated
to
Our Ultimate Source

Contents

Section III: On Religion and Beliefs

Appendices

Acknowledgments

FOR TWENTY YEARS I've been compiling notes to write a book. Another twenty years might have elapsed but for an authoress, Jeanette Jacot, who volunteered to help and encourage my writing. I sincerely thank her and all who helped type the rough drafts. My profound thanks to Stanley Hall, Helga Wood, and Marcia Walthrop for computerizing it.

I extend my sincere appreciation to Marianne Young for editing this manuscript and to Corinn Codye for refining it. A special thanks goes to Lee McCourry for his interest and help, and for the use of his office and equipment. My gratitude also extends to the Love Project, c/o The Teleos Institute in Arizona, as well as to the hundreds of other teachers throughout history upon whose wisdom I have drawn and thereby have come to recognize my Spiritual Nature as the Source and Creator of this book, which I humbly co-create. Finally, I want to thank you, the public, for your interest. I hope you will enjoy the benefits of living the principles enclosed, to enhance your personal world to overflowing, and thereby contribute in your own way to making our planet a better home in which to live.

In the Beginning

IN THE FIRST SECTION OF THIS BOOK, Peace shares his experiences as Peace Pilgrim II, as well as principles that he learned in the last thirty years of searching to make his life work and to find inner peace. He invites you to select what works for you to enhance your joy, understanding, and happiness.

The second section focuses on the process of understanding who and what we are, and living Peace. You may wish to read it as a self-help book of accumulated wisdoms, or choose to gather family, friends, and use it as a manual to facilitate a growth group. It is designed to share ideas for contemplation and to open the door for discussion, continuous awareness, and expansion of yourselves and one another.

The third section concentrates on religious and spiritual beliefs and is arranged to be used in a similar manner to Section II.

Preface

WHEN MAKING CHANGES, we tend to need to be reminded of various principles often, as they are new tools, reinforcing our desire to change. You may find some of these repeated throughout the book. Sometimes seeing them in another context is an "Aha, Now I get it!" situation.

When we choose to apply unconditional love as a way of life, we will indeed be on the way to Utopia. By sharing some of my walk experiences, I hope to uncover what life's all about, and how and why we might choose to improve it by combining our Spiritual Nature's insights with practical, down-to-earth methods. The aim is to oil the wheel of life, that it may flow more smoothly, roll further with less effort, and cover greater distances in less time.

We will look at our fear, insecurity, and lack of self-esteem, and discover how to accept and love ourselves so that we will no longer feel the need to explode into tempers, or flee into the painful escapes of drugs, alcoholism, self-deception, or pride, but rather gain the strength and understanding to express greater joy in our lives. By delving into the causes of fear, we can overcome its hold on us. By examining the ego, we can discover its constructive and destructive traits, enabling us to decide what to do with it. This book shows us how to disagree without being disagreeable, resentful, or hating.

Sometimes taking a good look at the motives for our behavior can give us clues about life, what is wrong with our approach to life, how to change, and the benefits of changing. We can expand the joy of living by recognizing our mistakes, correcting them, and growing away from *guilty* pasts. It is necessary to love ourselves before we can properly love others. Only then does love start to break down all the barriers and bring happiness into our lives and the lives of others.

So, if you're searching for a spiritual "something," I offer you a shortcut of spiritual hors d'oeuvres, which, had they been available to me in the form of this book, might have saved me a lot of frustration, time, and struggle. However, I have no regrets.

I offer powerful principles that enable you to solve your own problems. My aim here is to simplify a process, to bring you from where you are to where you want to be, more quickly. It is for you to choose what is going to work best for you. Accept or reject whatever inspires you.

I encourage you to move from negatives such as:

Fear

Guilt

Stress

Distress

Despair

Desperation

Distrust

Loneliness

Resentment

Poor eating habits

Bad health habits

Neglect of family

Child abuse

Physical or mental abuse

Temper and violence

Alcohol abuse

Smoking

Drug abuse

TOWARD

THE

POSITIVES

OF:

Self-Esteem

Integrity

Ethics
Communication
Love
Understanding
Awareness
Understanding of personal and business relationships
Putting yourself in charge of your life
with formulas that will help you overcome
all sorts of problems,
not just solutions to one particular one.

A few words of clarification.

I believe the Spirit of God to be all-inclusive and all-encompassing. To emphasize our inclusiveness, I use words such as Creator, Spiritual Power, Spiritual Nature, Spiritual Self, Spiritual Inner Guidance, Spiritual Essence, Higher Consciousness, Universal Power, Universal Nature, the Energy Force, the Eternal, and, very respectfully, It. For me these descriptions refer to the All-Knowing, timeless Creator of everything that is, was, or ever will be.

I would suggest that you please substitute your Word/s of reverence in place of mine. As an example, where I would say, "The Spiritual Essence is within me," you may, according to your belief, wish to read this as:

"Jesus is always with me," or,

"The power of The Great Spirit is with me," or,

"God is with me."

Any reference in this book to *good* versus *bad* or *evil* refers to positive versus negative, with *evil* meaning mistakes. Also, the word *love* has many connotations. In this book it mainly means kindness, consideration, compassion, caring, encouragement, self-esteem, joyfulness, contentment, and appreciation of our Spiritual Nature and of all creation. Also, when I refer to the Ego, this means the personality of the "little self," rather than the "Spiritual Self," which is the Universal power within us, the Energy force, the Eternal.

I write in very simple lay language to help you absorb and use the principles in your daily lives, to ease you into an harmonious, loving, and exciting adventure that you can effectively create. You are in the driver's seat of your life. Your freedom of choice and your imagination will guide you to follow your own drummer and give you the courage to do so.

A word of caution: I feel it is important that we view all spiritual and religious teachers and gurus as people who are signposts or guides that we may choose to follow, but without giving them our minds. We need to control and always be in charge of our own minds and beliefs, and not allow any person, group, or peers to govern our actions. We need to maintain a healthy balance between independence and interdependence.

Introduction

THE ORIGINAL PEACE PILGRIM, a woman, gave up all of her belongings and, without a penny, left Pasadena, California on January 1, 1953 to embark upon a walk of peace that lasted for twenty-eight years. In the first eleven years, she had walked 25,000 miles. Ironically, in 1981, while being driven to deliver a lecture, she was involved in a car accident and was killed. After her death, friends compiled a book of her talks and experiences, entitled *Peace Pilgrim,* and also a booklet called *Steps Toward Inner Peace,* from the text of her talks. Both are available, free, from Friends of Peace Pilgrim, 43480 Cedar Avenue, Hemet, California, 92544. (909) 927-7678. Should you want any of those booklets, I'm sure they'd be happy to send them to you. And if you'd like to make a donation, I'm sure they'd appreciate it.

On October 2, 1989, Peace Pilgrim II began in his unique way to follow her incredibly large footsteps to perpetuate peace. He gave up all of his possessions and also travelled without a penny, neither did he accept money from anyone. He relied upon people for food and shelter, otherwise he fasted or slept out. In his first year, he walked 2,000 miles and spoke at universities and churches, with religious leaders, mayors, city councils, and various groups including thousands of children at all levels of schooling. He was given extensive coverage in TV talk-shows, news, newspapers, magazine articles, and radio programs. He believes that peace has to begin with the individual, that we need to develop responsibility for our own actions, and that helpful, important tools to acquire are understanding, unconditional love, and abundant self-esteem, balanced by humility and the honesty to realize that although our spiritual beingness is perfect, our outer behavior or personality may require some improvement. He believes that if we sincerely want peace, we can obtain it, providing we're prepared to make the necessary changes to actually become peaceful, and *not merely to talk about it.*

All peace begins with each of us practicing simple truths, such as the Golden Rule of "Do unto others as you would have them do unto you." The way that we interact each day, especially with our families, leads either towards peace or hostility. We might start by asking ourselves on a daily basis, "Which am I personally contributing to, peace or conflict?" The way we behave affects others, and it benefits everyone as we develop positive attitudes. Learning to dissolve hatred with love may not seem easy, but it works. Most of us have learned from experience that meeting anger with anger only perpetuates the problem, magnifying it into a power struggle that nobody wins.

SECTION ONE

Enjoying the Journey

CHAPTER ONE

Becoming Peace Pilgrim

I WAS BORN IN London, England, and was brought up on the Island of Jersey, off the coast of France. We were very fortunate that in June, 1940, we left Jersey for England, because five days later the Germans occupied the Island. I remained in England throughout the war and was blessed to survive the bombing without a scratch. I started serving an apprenticeship as a diamond cutter. I then spent a couple of years in the Royal Air Force. In 1948, my wife and I left for South Africa, where we remained for five years, and I returned to cutting diamonds. Both my sons were born in Capetown, which is a beautiful city. However, we were interested in coming to the United States of America.

By 1954, we were living in California, where I learned all aspects of the jewelry business. In those days, although I had a pretty good life, it was marred by my ignorance. I wanted peace at any price and thought that being humble meant to be a doormat. In a highly competitive country, that meant a lot of frustration, as people took advantage of my weakness, and I found myself pushed until I burst into tempers, only to feel guilty and frustrated that I, who wanted peace, was demonstrating hostility.

In 1960, I started searching to grow and improve my life. I read many self-help books, studied comparative religions, and was on a merry-go-round of growthful meetings. At one such meeting, I met and spent several hours with an incredible woman, Peace Pilgrim. I thought that the work she was doing was important, and I knew that was her way of working for peace. My way, at the time, was much less dramatic and far more comfortable!

In 1975, after a two year illness, my wife died. I shed many tears and much pain in the few months that followed. Then, while shaving one day, the realization hit me that what I was doing was pulling myself and my family down. I was not really crying for my wife, because I realized that she'd graduated to a higher plateau, and was no longer suffering on this physical plane. I was crying for myself because of the awareness of being without her for the rest of my life. I decided it was time to live for the living, and though the love remains, the grieving time was over.

For years I had wanted to get out of the business world but felt trapped, because I had financial obligations to provide for my family and did not know how I could support them if I left my profession. What else could I do to provide an income if I didn't have other skills? I did have other skills, and I enjoyed working with people and giving spiritual counseling, but that was not income producing. My sons were now adults, so I decided that I no longer had family responsibilities. I would, within a five-year period, resign my position as the manager of a large, wholesale diamond company and change my life-style, so that I could work with people, which is what I did.

By 1987, I was living semiretired in Eugene, Oregon, doing volunteer work as a crisis counselor, facilitating groups, enjoying my life, friends, and a very comfortable *comfort zone*. I appreciate nature's beauty and usually walked a few miles a day to enjoy it, while at the same time exercising my body. For about eighteen months, I lived this blissful life-style.

One day, while walking, it was as if my mind was thinking and gently saying, "You're to be Peace Pilgrim." It was so gentle that I ignored it at first, thinking, "That's a funny thought. I suppose next I'll be told to go to the moon!" I continued walking, forgetting the incident. However, it was soon to occur again. This time the message was a little firmer: "You're to be Peace Pilgrim."

Then, shortly afterwards again, it came even more firmly. All at once I got the message: this isn't imagination, this is real. I panicked and, within my head, began a ping-pong game of thoughts.

"You're to be Peace Pilgrim."

"No, I don't want to be Peace Pilgrim. I'm happy here, doing what I enjoy. I have friends, I enjoy my life and my new car, just the way it is."

Very strong now, "You're to be Peace Pilgrim."

I fought this idea for ten days and nights, but finally, reluctantly, and not too graciously, I gave in to it. What were my thoughts and feelings during that time? Well, first panic, then resistance, and gradually the realization that this was going to happen. The old me was going to disappear into a new name, closing off the past and going pennilessly into the future. Talk about *out on a limb!* I was a city person, not used to camping out. Yet one thing kept going through my mind, "Not my will, but thine, be done." And then, "How am I going to explain this to my sons?"

I did explain it to them. I called my son in California. He listened to what I had to say and was totally against the idea, being very concerned for my safety traffic-wise. Even more so, he said, "There are lots of crazies out there; can't you find another way of expressing your peace views?" We talked some more, and eventually he said, "I know you're going to do what you say you're going to do, and nothing I say will change your mind, but at least don't get rid of all your things. Rent out the apartment for a few months, and see how things go." I explained that it would be too easy to give up and return if I didn't burn my bridges. So, everything had to go.

I could feel his frustration and concern for my safety, and I realized what my feelings might have been had the circumstances been reversed. I told him that I understood his views and feelings, and that I loved him dearly, but that like him, I had to live my life my way. He understood. I asked him not to say anything to his brother, as I wanted to break it to him personally, having previously arranged to spend a couple weeks with him in Canada. I called ahead of time to let him know the time I'd arrive, and said that I'd decided to go travelling and would fill him in with the details when I saw him.

When I arrived, he was curious as to what was happening, so I shared the details with him. He immediately wanted to know what his brother had said and, of course, basically agreed with him.

Several times during the visit he suggested I reconsider, but my mind was made up.

I enjoyed my stay and got ready for the six weeks of preparation I now faced before leaving Eugene. Several of my friends sided with my sons' views, but one friend, Bill Wilson, a Unity Minister, was very encouraging and I think more than a little envious, but he had a young family to consider, so he was delighted that, at least, I was going to do it.

I decided to leave Eugene at the beginning of October, before the weather got too cold. This gave me six weeks in which to give away or sell off my possessions and purchase the essentials for my journey. The original Peace Pilgrim merely carried with her a hair brush and a toothbrush, but I felt the need to at least start off with a sleeping bag, extra underwear, and a change of warm clothes and jacket, as well as a tent and shaving equipment. All of these things I fit into a duffel bag, and towed on a dolly that I had converted into a form of rickshaw, and my sons inherited what was left.

Whereas I agree with Peace Pilgrim's message and plan to perpetuate it as best I can, I am also aware that each of us is unique, and we have to be true to ourselves. She was a walker and used to country living and survival. I was a city person, not so versed. She spoke mainly to universities and churches. I was to find myself talking most often to schools. The important thing, I feel, is not our differences, but our purpose, that of spreading peace.

About a week before my journey started, I took a couple of friends out to lunch, while I still had the money! In conversation, one of them said, "You know, Peace, when you leave here, you take your friends with you." Those words were to ring true and to fortify me often in the months ahead. Then she said something which became an incredible spiritual breakthrough for me. She said, "And you know, Peace, when you walk out there for peace, you'll be walking for millions of people." Instantly, my humble mind jumped in with, "Millions of people? I can't do that. Millions of people? I . . ." But before I could think any more, a strong, firm inner voice said, "It's not you doing it!"

Suddenly, I felt very confident, gentle but strong and capable, and for the first time I personally realized the meaning of "Don't hide your light under a bushel." From that moment on, I was able to go humbly but confidently, firm, knowing that the Power within me would always be there to express through me. And it has and still does.

This has made my work a joy, as I share with people that this incredible Power is not exclusive to me, but what's true for me is true for everyone. Don't hide your uniqueness. It's your gift to share. Know that you can do it. Trust in the Universal Power, and do it. Don't hide your light under a bushel, you're precious, and you can do it.

I had planned to increase my daily conditioning walk from three to five miles, maybe ten or twelve, but with so much going on— divesting myself of my belongings, shopping, learning to use camp equipment, bidding farewell to friends, and all those last minute details—instead of increasing the walk, I had to completely cancel it. Therefore, when I started out on October 2, 1989, it was without any walking practice.

I arrived in downtown Eugene about five minutes late, as media and friends were there to see me off at nine o'clock. I apologized for being late, as I no longer had a car. I felt very emotional, seeing all my friends there to walk with me a ways, and I broke down, crying and hugging them all as the TV camera captured my tears.

The walk began, and after a few miles, some of the well-wishers had to drop off and return to their jobs and homes. After about eight miles, the last of the friends left for a prearranged ride back, and I was alone. How did that feel? Luckily, I remembered the words, "When you leave here, Peace, you take your friends with you." That felt really good, and also I began to feel a tinge of excitement as I realized that I was going to meet new and as yet unknown friends along the way. I got to Junction City and visited Wade Skinner, the craftsman who revamped my cart for me. I felt that the handlebars were too short, cramping my shoulders, and asked if he could extend them for me as a favor, for I no longer had money to pay him. Not only did he delight in doing it, but insisted that I stay overnight. The first night out, and I was in a bed! That felt good, not to mention dinner and breakfast the next morning, before I really started my journey off alone as Peace Pilgrim II.

Before proceeding further with my journey, I'd like to share in some more detail how I feel I'd developed the traits of people pleasing, tempers, guilt, and hostility, and more important, how I was able to learn to overcome them.

I was brought up to be loving and humble and to me, at the time, "humble" meant everyone was better than me, and that my opinions were not even worthy of consideration, and that loving meant to keep the peace and give in, rather than be heard and create confrontation. Imagine the frustration of trying to live this way as people, recognizing my sign of "Kick Me," obliged. I felt, and was, constantly taken advantage of. My *love* kept me dishonestly acting nicely on the outside while burning up on the inside. Unlike a train, I did not have a safety valve, so that when the pressure built up I would try, humbly and weakly, to warn *them* to stop, as *they* were annoying me. If they failed to heed the warning, I'd suddenly explode into a violent temper, which I'd keep going as a lesson to *them* not to do it again. How pathetic that I was so weak, and gave them permission to control my life, but at the time, I didn't know any better. Now, having exploded, my *loving me* was frustrated at my behavior, and I felt guilt-ridden.

I remained a victim for years, but inside me, I knew something was wrong, this was not the way to live, so I began searching. I was now in my thirties, and while I was participating in an encounter group, the facilitator, talking to one of the other participants, said, "You don't have to be a victim of circumstances. You have choices. You can take responsibility and control your own life. You no longer need to be a slave to others." At that, I burst out crying for about ten minutes. All those years of pain could have been avoided had I known that I could make choices.

Here, I'd like to share some thoughts about a baby that is molded into a particular pattern through the influence of parents, teachers, and daily experience, as well as by the genes inherent in him. His/her character is quite formed by the time s/he is five or six years old.

In the early teens s/he is likely to have experienced likes and dislikes, attitudes, opinions, conflicts of interest and action, sometimes helplessness, hopelessness, and giving up, and through these growing experiences, teenage rebellion. I learned that in our teens, we're usually the product of our environment, and we blame people, places, and things for our predicaments. Some of us keep thinking that way all of our lives. I did that till I was thirty-five. But there is such a thing as *behavioral change*, and once we know that, we can discover that the clay baby that is being molded into whatever age we are, has not been fired up and hardened solid, but is still pliable and can be changed to fit any mold.

What is most important to know is that we are the mold makers. We can make anything out of our lives from now on, because unlike any other animals, we have been given the marvelous gift of "freedom of choice." Until we know this, we go through life blaming and accusing everyone else for our fate, for, seemingly, we have to react to life and put up with the consequences. Once we know that we have choices, we can choose to stop blaming others for what they have done to us and accept responsibility for our own lives, wisdom, and understanding.

I learned to be honest with myself and others, and how to become assertive, not aggressive. I learned the art of conflict resolution. This really is essential to discover, for it enables us to engage verbally with people without the need for violence or fear. You become able to express your feelings in a nonthreatening way. I'll explain more about it in a chapter that's in section two of this book.

With my needs met, I was able to take control of my life, to let go of the temper-causing frustration and resultant guilts. If you've experienced any victim-like feelings, take hope. There is a way out. So, read on.

CHAPTER TWO

Walking for Peace

I WAS NOW STARTING the second day of my walk. I towed my rickshaw cart with the words "Peace Pilgrim II" on it, dressed in a shirt, sweater, pants, covered with a zippered jacket and a lettered tunic with the words "Peace Pilgrim II" on the front and "Walking for Peace" on the back, and I was trying out my newly-extended handlebars, hoping that they'd work. My journey was to take me through Corvallis to Salem, then, after seeing the Governor of the state of Oregon, west to Lincoln City, south along the coast to California, Los Angeles, San Diego, and then east to New York. That was my plan, my only plan.

Suddenly I realized that Peace Pilgrim was more than just a walk. What was I supposed to do? With all of the hustle and bustle of the last six weeks, I'd not taken time to think this through. Although I'd spent time with Peace Pilgrim twenty-two years earlier, I was concerned that, other than having read her book, I knew nothing of how she survived, nor had I any directions to follow. I was totally reliant on my Spiritual Power and did not feel my faith was strong enough to cope. Even though deep inside I knew to trust my Universal Power, doing so in these conditions was something else. I decided to make the best of it and enjoy the walk. The handlebars were working great, and I was able to move my hands along them to balance the weight on the wheels rather than using my arms and back as I had had to on the first day. The weather was cool and ideal for walking. Oregon is such a beautiful state, and its scenery is one of my delights. I felt good. As the Chinese say, "A journey of a thousand miles begins with just one step." So I made the choice to live one day at a time. I knew that I could handle that, especially as I'd been given food for the road and knew at least where my lunch meal was coming from!

The second day was a day of great surprises and insight for me. I'd been walking for about three hours when a car, coming from behind, pulled over, and one of my friends got out. She'd come out to see me, to see how I was doing, and to let me know that she and her son would meet me later on that evening at a small town further ahead and take me to dinner. This was really a morale booster, that someone would drive all the way out to find me, return to Eugene, and then come back later to treat me to dinner. It's no wonder the original Peace Pilgrim kept saying, "People are wonderful."

After she left that afternoon, I was enjoying my walk, looking forward to the evening, when the second surprise occurred. About two hundred yards away on the opposite side of the street I saw a barn or a shed, and two dogs were there; they saw me and started barking profusely. One of them started running towards me, probably provoked by my rickshaw. I had a metal bar that I used as a tripod for my cart so I could sit and rest when necessary. For a brief second I thought of using it to defend myself, but violence was not an option for me. So instead I decided to keep walking and look straight ahead, ignoring the dog and putting my trust in the Universal Power.

From the corner of my eye, I saw the dog coming up onto the other side of the highway to attack me. It was still barking when suddenly I heard a thud, and the animal lay dead a few feet from my right side. It was instant death—no blood, no mess, just as if it had laid down to go to sleep. What had happened was that a small truck coming from behind hadn't seen the dog in time to brake as the animal suddenly appeared on the highway, and consequently the driver couldn't prevent the accident. I felt sorry for this because I like animals, but it was being hostile. This, on only my second day out, taught me that truly I can always depend on Universal Power for protection, even though earthly logic pointed to my being attacked. It was a demonstration of faith that I'll never forget, even though I'd later find myself needing more faith as I proceeded on my journey.

My friends who had journeyed out to take me to dinner met me in daylight, and we had a leisurely dinner. By the time that was over, it was dark. When they returned home, I stood outside the restaurant. *Now what?* I spotted a market nearby and saw at the end of the parking lot what appeared to be a field. I walked over and decided to pitch my tent at the end of the parking lot, where it seemed to be flat. There was barely enough room in the tent for me and my duffel bag, so my pushcart stayed outside. In the morning I got up and started to break down my tent, which was white with frost, as was my rickshaw. I was about halfway through, just ready to drop my tent, when a police car approached, and out got a burly sergeant, asking what I was doing there, because a patrolman had reported my being there and the station was so concerned that he had come out personally to investigate. I explained the details of who I was, why I was there, and apologized for any inconvenience I may have caused. He was adamant that I should have notified them, in case something happened to me without them even knowing I was in town. Then, just as abruptly, he had a change of heart, saw that I was about ten minutes from leaving, and wished me luck.

I walked about fifteen miles and realized that the soles of my feet were getting warm. I still had seven miles to go to Corvallis, and I decided I could walk that okay. I did make it to Corvallis and was walking past a market parking lot when a woman drove by, parked her car, and walked over to me. Having read the original Peace Pilgrim's book, she connected me with her and came over to talk and see if I had any food or accommodations. I said that I had neither, as I had just arrived. She invited me and my belongings into her car, and we drove a few miles to a church, where she introduced me to people who became my hosts, not just for a night as I had intended, but for a week.

During the next few days my feet were badly blistered, and I was hobbling along one day, trying to figure out what to do. There was a high school nearby, so I decided to go there and see if they'd be interested in my sharing with the students about my walk for peace, about how important it is for young people to learn peaceful ways of living, for what we practice, we become. Fortunately, a teacher was open to my suggestion, and almost immediately I found myself addressing my first high school class, and realized that this appealed to me, and to the classroom, so I decided to place school visits high on my priority list.

I was offered a ride to Salem, but felt that if I had "Walking for Peace" on my tunic, I should walk and not ride. However, my feet were too blistered, so I did accept the ride. In Salem I became the guest of Willamette University for a few days, where I enjoyed giving talks and sharing with students. I also walked across the street to the capitol building to see the Governor. I was informed by his secretary that he'd been out of town and was just in for a day before leaving again the next day. His schedule was tight, and without an appointment there was no way I could get to see him. Just then, the door opened, and out he came to greet other dignitaries. He saw me, we smiled, and at least I was able to leave a message. I decided later to visit and speak to many city council meetings and mayors along the way, to let them know that at the schools I'd visited, all the children I'd asked wanted peace, and that I felt that they were sincere about living it.

I spoke with people from the Oregon Peace Group and suggested to the Chamber of Commerce that they plant a Peace Pole in their Peace Garden near the library, inviting the Governor, Mayor, and other dignitaries, as well as the media, to attend. I haven't followed through to see if it's happened. All I can do is to make recommendations and hope that they materialize. I cannot allow myself to get caught up in the results. I believe that if it's meant to be, it'll happen, if not now, hopefully in the not-too-distant future.

It was now time to leave Salem and head for the coast. Unfortunately, I didn't have a local map, and after many inquiries I was unable to find a side road out of the city. I supposed there must be one, but I was unable to find it. So, putting my trust in my Spiritual Power, I walked along the edge of the freeway. Cars were whizzing by, and when trucks went past me, the wind created by them as they passed almost took me with them. At the second off-ramp, I decided that there must be a parallel road nearby, so I raced across and off the ramp. I came to a Texaco station and talked to the attendant, asking him for a spot of oil for my rickshaw wheels. He thought that I was "plain crazy," walking across the country without money, even if it was for peace. I shared that he was entitled to his opinion, that this was my calling, and that I was beginning to enjoy it.

Continuing my journey, I walked on and found a field to sleep in. The next day, I walked past a garden where an apple tree had dropped many delicious apples on the road side of the fence. I was able to load about ten of them with my things, which was as much room as I had for them. I walked about seven and a half hours that day and ate lots of apples. By mid-afternoon I was hungry, but just couldn't eat another apple. I walked past an all-you-can-eat restaurant and would have liked a couple of eggs on toast. However, without money, that was not possible. So, onward!

I decided I needed to walk five more miles that day, as I wanted to get to the coast in time to visit a church there on Sunday morning, and was afraid that, as it was a hilly area, I might not make it in time. After about two miles, I began to think that maybe I'd made a mistake about continuing further, that it would soon be dusk, and that the roadside offered no place for a tent. Just about that time, I thought I heard a call. I looked back and saw a lady walking up the hill, trying to catch me. I walked back towards her, and we talked about the original Peace Pilgrim, and about what I was doing.

She invited me back down the hill to meet her husband, who had parked their motorhome in the driveway of somebody's field. She wanted pictures and a story for her organization's newsletter, and then said, "We're about to have dinner and you're invited." There, in the middle of the country, she cooked steaks in the motorhome. I didn't get the eggs on toast that I'd wanted, but I got a dinner instead. I'm not much of a meat eater anymore, for health reasons and for ecological purposes, but it did taste good. I've come to accept miracles like this as a norm.

Lest that statement should sound smug, let me mention that despite the lesson of faith the attacking dog had taught me, I found that during my first month out I spent most of my energy concerned about where I would get my next meal. It nearly always showed up somehow, but it made me realize that I needed to pray for additional faith, even though deep inside I already knew to trust my Spiritual Self. I'm not proud of the fact that I had a lack of trust, but the truth is, despite everything working for me, I still felt that I was lacking faith. I sometimes wonder what it takes before we are completely trusting. I guess perhaps it's a constant challenge for us to keep growing.

You may be wondering, since we're not allowed to talk religion in the schools, just what I'd shared with the high school students. Well, I told them about the original Peace Pilgrim, and how she travelled for twenty-eight years, plus a little bit about myself—how I'd become involved, and that my message is, "Peace begins with me, each one of us." It involves living the Golden Rule, "Do unto others as you'd have them do to you," and requires that we change hatred with love—love being understanding, caring, listening, sharing, respecting, and not using force or retaliation, but communicating. I shared that we become what we practice. As we practice living peacefully, which means living fully, not just sitting on the sidelines, we bring peace into the world. If we practice hostility, we create conflict, which, as adults, creates wars.

One of the reasons for unacceptable behavior is a lack of self-esteem. Another is frustration, through not knowing how to handle situations that come up in life. Let's deal first with self-esteem and see what it is and how it affects us. Self-esteem is what we come to believe about ourselves as a result of our surrounding influences. Unfortunately, most of us have been brought up in dysfunctional homes.

It's not that the people are bad, but rather they have passed down to us mistakes that they've learned from their parents and grandparents, so that you might be told, for example, "Tidy up your room. You're untidy. You'll never amount to anything. You're no good. You're always, ta da . . . ta da . . . ta da . . .," all the things that are negative.

Unfortunately, these people have not separated you from your action. You see, your action or behavior may not be acceptable. But you are a precious, wonderful, unique human being with an incredible potential to do wondrous things, but what you came to believe is a lie that you're no good. If you really believe that, how do you feel? Usually not too good about yourself, and if you don't feel good, how do you behave? Usually not too good.

On the other hand, if you've been taught that you're an okay person, you usually have a high self-esteem, feel good about yourself, and behave accordingly. Advertisers out to sell their products try to influence you that you're not good enough if you don't buy their lipstick, their eye makeup, their perfume, their hair cream, and their designer clothes. The truth is, you're okay without them. If you want those things for preference, that's fine, but it's not going to make you any better, for you're spiritually perfect already. All you need to do is bring your actions and behavior into harmony with your perfection. Your conscience is your inner guide that lets you know if you're on the right track or not.

If, for example, you have been brought up in an alcoholic family, rather than learning to follow the wrong pathway, you may learn from it that that's definitely not the way you want to live your life, and as you're now maturing, you can learn more constructive behavior.

You can make choices and choose to do anything you wish. But remember, everything has an effect. Life is like a mirror, sooner or later it returns to you what you put out. So I suggest you seek peace, love, joy, and all the nice things you enjoy about your friends, like honesty, dependability, a sense of humor, and integrity. But to have a friend we need to be one. As we start to live this way, we'll learn how to handle life satisfactorily.

CHAPTER THREE

"People are Wonderful"

WE'D FINISHED DINNER in the motorhome. It was already dark, so I did accept the offer of the eighteen-mile ride to Lincoln City, where we arrived at about nine o'clock. I immediately tried to call a contact that I'd been given there. This would be an easy task under normal circumstances, but when travelling without money I have to seek the help of a local business to use their phone. This gives me an opportunity to explain my mission, but even so, it's an humbling experience, and then, having a phone doesn't guarantee that the person I'm calling is home. There wasn't anybody home!

I decided to walk a couple of miles to a deserted state park and spend the night there. The next day was a repeat performance, with nobody at home. Usually when I arrive at a town I seek out schools, churches, city councils, and the media to present my message, but most of these were unavailable on Saturdays, so I walked into town to get exposure and see what might happen.

By 2:30 in the afternoon I was pretty cold and hungry and decided a silent prayer would be in order. So I said to my Spiritual Power, "You've got me here, you want me here, I don't know what I'm to do. I need help." Nothing happened! I couldn't just stand in the doorway, so I decided to keep walking. After I walked about a hundred and fifty yards, a white station wagon pulled up. A lady got out of it and looked as if she wanted to say something. I stopped, said "Hello," and found that she'd read Peace Pilgrim's book and was surprised to see a man in her stead. I briefly explained that I was trying to perpetuate her cause. We talked for about a minute, and she asked, "Do you have a place to stay?" When I told her that I did not, she said, "Put your things in the back of my station wagon. I'm going to be out of town for four days. Meanwhile, my house is yours." One moment I was in the street, cold and hungry, the next in a house with two large windows overlooking the ocean, and food! When things like this keep happening in answer to my prayers, and even without them, as in the case the day before when in the middle of the country, out of nowhere, I'm suddenly cooked a dinner, I begin to realize that miracles are normal.

I don't often pray, per se, but perpetually delight in the Spiritual Nature's wondrous gifts. The whole of nature is given to us free, and it's awesome. I'm constantly inspired by the sunset or a sunrise, by the enormous variety of plants and the splendor of trees housing such a variety of birds, the beauty of the calm and sometimes wild ocean, and the elegance of a seagull gracefully and effortlessly gliding by. I feel that my appreciation is a constant prayer and feel blessed that I trust the Universal Power and the good in all of life.

I rely entirely upon Its love for my well-being and for my talks. I couldn't memorize one to save my life, yet they keep coming from the heart, naturally. I keep meeting new friends, and without a penny I feel as if I'm as rich as a millionaire, and without their worries or fears of losing their material wealth. I enjoy the great outdoors, even though most of my life was spent in cities, yet I also enjoy the comforts of a shower, a cozy room, and a washing machine when possible. I see nothing wrong with a little luxury, providing we own the things and they don't own us, but I feel that hoarding or greed is cumbersome and tends to take away from the real values, wherein lie the greatest happiness.

On Sunday I did make it to the church and spent the day with people I met there. Monday morning, I was at the local newspaper office before 9:00 A.M. having an interview. Upon leaving their office, I was walking into town to see if I could get on the local radio station's one-hour hot-line talk show, when a red car passed and honked. I waved acknowledgment. When I got to the radio station, I was met with a, "Hello, this is the second time I've seen you today. I was driving the red car. Come, I want to introduce you to the radio host." A few minutes later I was being asked to return for the 11:00 A.M. program. They had recently changed the program from 8:00 to 11:00 A.M. and needed a guest speaker for their hot-line talk show. On my way out I was introduced to the news commentator, who invited me to be on the news, also.

With one hour left until that appointment, I walked up the hill to a school and arranged with the principal of the school to spend the following day there talking to children in several of their classrooms. I really like people and am especially fond of children. They are so fresh, eager, and open to learn. They're still in touch with their feelings and know when they are loved. In the ensuing months I was privileged to share the message of peace with thousands of school-children.

I returned to the radio station, and after the program, waiting for me as I left the studio, was the lady I had been trying to contact. She'd gotten back into town, heard the program on her car radio, and stopped by to take me to lunch. When I left her, I visited a TV station and was interviewed for their news program. It is very exciting to be able to reach so many people and remind them of their preciousness. I spent the next few days talking at the schools and was invited by one of the teachers to have dinner and stay with her family at their home in Depoe Bay on my way south to Newport.

I left Lincoln City that Friday afternoon. The weather was very stormy, and the seagulls seemed to be floating stationary in the wind, or gliding gracefully wherever it took them. The sea was very turbulent and beautiful. The clouds were whizzing by, creating constantly changing patterns. It was a day to walk fast and keep the circulation moving. I arrived at Depoe Bay at about 5:30 P.M. to discover that my hosts had also invited friends from Newport to dinner, so that we could all meet and socialize. It's interesting how quickly strangers can come together and become lasting friends. Most people want to do this but are too shy or reserved, so it takes us being the initiators. What seems to prevent us is the fear of being rejected. It's been my experience that people are only too happy to respond once the ice has been broken, and, with the very few who may not want to do that, I have the opportunity to respect their privacy, and not take it as a personal rejection. My new Newport friends contacted their local peace group and notified them that I would be arriving on Saturday, and they made arrangements for accommodations. When I left Depoe Bay, the storm had worsened. It was cold, windy, and very wet. As I expressed my thanks and said good-bye to my hosts, they produced a large bag of delicious food, including homemade cake, so I didn't have to be concerned about food on that part of the journey. However, when I arrived in Newport, I was really cold, hungry, and soaking wet. My new hosts put on a bowl of soup, and while that was heating, offered me a hot bath. I remember that bath. The water was so hot that I came out of it sweating. I had the soup, yet was still cold. It was as if the cold had settled into the marrow of my bones. It took about half an hour for me to thaw out!

I was complemented for my perfect timing, but actually I had no idea that my arrival coincided with a Japanese delegation from Hiroshima, who were here to promote peace and never, ever again to use atomic bombs. Since some of them were miraculous survivors, they told their stories at the schools. I was fortunate to join that delegation and share the day with them, also to share my message with the schools. That evening, the peace group hosted a dinner for us all, and presentations were made to the mayor and received from him, while the media covered the whole story.

Next day, towing my cart, I left to continue on my journey south, walking the narrow coastal roads and breathing in the magnificent sea air, as well as the spectacular scenery. Occasionally, logging trucks would speed by, and as with my freeway experience, the wind vacuum that they produced would almost sweep me in with them. Sometimes people would stop and talk, take pictures, or offer me money, which I appreciated but did not accept. However, I was very happy to accept any accommodations that were offered as well as any food made available to me. It was raining pretty constantly, and along my journey a lady stopped her car and offered me accommodations a few hundred yards down the street. It felt so good to get in the warmth and have a hot shower, share some of my experiences, and get some rest before beginning early the next day with similar weather conditions.

In Yachats, I met a storekeeper who organized and arranged for me a house all to myself for the night, while the storm raged on. Next morning I awakened to beautiful weather and continued on to Florence. I was pleased that it had turned out sunny; it added to the beauty of the incredible coastal view. In Florence, I had secured newspaper coverage, and one of the schools had me in the gym all day long sharing with group after group of children, as two or three classes were brought in at a time. I really admire the principal for organizing the school upon such short notice and for his personal interest in having the children hear my message before I left town. He also saw to it that I had accommodations and provided me with food.

I walked on to Reedsport, where a local camping ground let me stay overnight. In the morning I was on my way to a school, when I saw police working with a minor accident. They were just finishing up with their detailed paperwork, when, as I drew near, the sergeant, who was very alert, stopped me for identification and information as to what I was doing there. He seemed satisfied that all was okay, and directed me to a school nearby, which I was my destination.

Once there, as on many previous occasions, I met with a very cooperative and friendly principal and staff of teachers. I spent the rest of the day sharing with wonderful children. It's such a delight to be with them—to see their interest, to hear their questions, and to hope that by substantiating their teacher's views on nonviolence, cooperation, and respect, that it may provide a guide whereby their lives run a little more smoothly and avoid some of the pitfalls that they might otherwise fall into.

My next stop was to be Coos Bay, and as the school principal lived there, I accepted the ride she offered and arrived there a day or two earlier than I had anticipated. I went to visit Ken Keyes College, where I'd been a student just a few years earlier. It was a fun reunion, and I was to remain their guest for the whole week while I lectured and mingled with the students, many of whom became friends and later accommodated me along my journey. I addressed the mayor and the city council and spoke to more schools and children, as well as at a church. At Ken Keyes College, two classes were ending that weekend, and I was offered rides by many people to go to Bandon.

Saturday morning, I left. The weather was particularly warm and beautiful, so I elected to walk to Bandon. Several of the students and instructors walked with me to the end of town; then I was once more on my own. I'd been treated to food and some nuts and raisins for the journey, and I was enjoying my walk, only to find students periodically stopping to offer me a ride. That made it even more fun, having visitors along the way. I continued walking, but ran out of water about eight miles from my destination. Pretty soon a car coming towards me did a U-turn, and the couple in it stopped to talk to me.

During the course of the conversation they wanted to support me with money. As usual, I thanked them but said that I only accepted food or accommodations, and occasional rides, and that I was walking on to Bandon. They directed me to the scenic route, neither of us realizing that it was a couple of miles longer that way! They said that they were going to get me some food and orange juice and would find me on the journey. And that's exactly what they did. Orange juice never tasted so good!

I finally arrived in Bandon, after walking thirty miles, the longest distance I ever walked, or ever will, in one day. I felt fine, other than a little dehydrated, so I headed for the first coffee shop in sight. It turned out to be a hostel, and I was greeted with, "We've been expecting you; you'll be our guest while you're here." Despite their generosity, I said that first I needed water, and then I'd come and talk to them. I downed what seemed like a quart of water before returning to inquire how they knew I was coming, and found that a Coos Bay newspaper article saying that I was headed that way had already reached their bulletin board. Until now, I had not experienced the need of exercising after walking. However, for the following two days, I was so stiff that I walked just like a gorilla.

While in Bandon, I visited the mayor, spoke at schools, and visited a kindergarten school that had Soviets visiting at the same time. We were all very impressed by the emphasis on cooperation, consideration, and communication that the school was competently teaching with incredible results. While still in Bandon, I met Daniel Dennel, and spent much time with him, seeing how he healed all the wild animals that had been brought to him. I was also hosted to lunch by a church member and given a tour of his cranberry farm. In general, I spent a happy, learning, and fulfilling week there.

After I left Bandon, I'd gone but a few miles when a car approaching me pulled over, and a mother and daughter, carrying a plateful of cupcakes, approached me. The mother explained that just yesterday I'd spoken to young children at school, and that her daughter had come home and told them about my visit. Today her sister, who was taking her birthday cakes over to a party, wanted me to have one. Is it any wonder that I love children, which brings me to an important point.

In his book, *The Prophet,* Kalhil Gibran states, "Your children are not your children. As parents, we've been given the privilege to bring them into the world, and to care for them." It is said that in the United States, eighty-five percent of the children are brought up in dysfunctional homes. It's as if we feel that we own the children and that they are objects or toys to be dealt with as we please, to abuse sexually, physically, verbally, and in other horrible ways. Perhaps we can learn that these children are of the Eternal Spirit of God, precious Royalty of the most high, to be respected, loved, and cared for as the treasures that they are. Most adults have been brought up by good intending parents, but have nevertheless been abused, and are still paying for it now. Free yourself by learning to forgive your parents, for they knew not what they did. They probably inherited poor parenting habits from their parents, but we must break the chain, get our priorities right, and start loving ourselves, and especially our children and relatives. If we can meet that challenge, strangers will be easy to deal with, by comparison.

By the way, you are also a precious, Regal baby, only grown up now. Develop your self-esteem, love yourself, and claim your Spiritual Inheritance. You'll then learn to recognize it in others, and to love that Spiritual Essence in them, too. They are spiritually perfect, but if they don't accept that for themselves, it may take a while before their outward behavior matches their inner beauty. Remember, they are not their actions, they are potential wonders waiting to happen, and so are we!

CHAPTER FOUR

Challenges and
Opportunities

I CONTINUED MY JOURNEY south and walked into Port Orford, where, borrowing somebody's telephone, I called a couple whose names I'd been given to contact there, but they were out. I walked to the senior citizens' meeting place, hoping to give a talk and perhaps get fed there. It was closed. By now it was about 2:30 in the afternoon, and I wondered what to do. As I started walking, I saw a sign indicating *scenic view*. I continued about halfway up the hill in that direction, when a man unloading a van, seeing me pushing a cart, came up to ask about my rickshaw and ask what "Peace Pilgrim" was all about. I told him what I was doing, and immediately he went for his wallet to support my efforts. I thanked him, but as on previous occasions I refused the money. He said, "Okay, then come on in, we're just about to eat."

Usually, at 3:30 on a Saturday afternoon, people don't sit down to dinner, but I believe the Universal Power was at work again with another miracle. They were eating early as they were leaving for an out of town visit. I enjoyed being with them, and the food was outstanding. Thus it was about an hour later that I continued up the hill, waddling to the top! When I reached the summit, I was treated to a lovely view of a small fishing area and a beautiful view of the coastline. So, if you're ever in the area of Port Orford, be sure to visit it.

I again called my contacts, who were now home, and made arrangements with them to pick me up. They spoiled me, housed me, and fed me for nearly a week, while I spoke at several local schools and was transported to others. What a privilege. It was almost Thanksgiving, and a friend drove down, about 600 miles round trip, to take me to friends to celebrate Thanksgiving. I've come to learn that the more one gives of oneself, the more comes back from completely unexpected sources. I had not wanted them to put themselves out like that, but they insisted, and a good time and a genuine Thanksgiving was had by all.

I was headed for Eureka, California, and was given a ride by a former school teacher who was going to Crescent City. Originally I thought he felt skeptical about me, but as we got engrossed in conversation, he said that he'd take me on to Eureka. I pointed out that that would be 160 miles round trip out of his way, but he insisted. When we arrived, I called a couple of teachers who were expecting me at sometime, but they were out. My ride insisted on taking me out to dinner, after which, when I again called to find my contact still out, he insisted on staying with me until they returned. I had great difficulty preventing him from doing so. Again, I think of the original Peace Pilgrim's words, "People are wonderful."

I was unable to contact the teachers, so I decided to see if I could find a meeting that I could attend. I found one, but I was so tired that I fell asleep through part of it. Despite that, a couple invited me to stay with them for a few days, and I finally reached my contact and was picked up by them almost immediately.

I stayed in Eureka and Arcata for about ten days, and during that time visited several schools, talking to about twelve hundred children. My host was the superintendent and principal of a school that had peace posters all over it, which made me feel very welcome. Visiting his wife's school, I was met at the main gate on a drizzling, foggy day by the principal, a woman, and several of the children holding a six-foot long banner of peace. In all the classrooms, as well as on the doors, were signs and paintings of peace that the children had worked on. I was extremely moved, had difficulty holding back tears, and it was almost too much to talk to them, as I was choked up. I carried this message to the mayor and the city council as well as in my heart.

I also spoke at several churches and got rides from one to the next, in order to get there in time for their services on the same day. By now the daytime temperature was down to about forty degrees, and quite damp, so I wanted to get further south. My hosts wanted me to remain with them through Christmas and offered to drive me to San Francisco afterwards. They had been strangers just a couple weeks before! The next day, other people who were driving to Los Angeles offered me a ride, so I decided to go partway with them to warmer weather. We got to San Francisco, and it was cold and damp there, too. So, being encouraged, I drove on with them to Los Angeles.

On my journey I've encountered many challenges and opportunities that crop up to be dealt with, some of which I've already mentioned—the attacking dog, dealing with blistered feet, deciding on (as Peace Pilgrim II) what I was meant to do, and how to keep fit in changing climates—but now came a new challenge. Travelling through smaller towns, it was relatively easy to get known and be on the media, or to get instant speaking engagements, but now, in the big city, with everyone driving, nobody saw me walking. The TV stations required more interesting news than one walking the country just for peace! I couldn't even get past the security guards to see the program personnel. Also, it was Christmas time, and schools were closed. I'd lived in the Los Angeles area, and even with a car, money, and a home, I'd found it too hectic. Now I wondered how I was going to manage.

Somebody bought me a monthly bus pass, so I could at least move around. The problem was, it took me three hours to get to my destination, giving me just a couple of hours to do the work before having to head back. I visited several churches and spoke briefly at some of them, and I did manage to get some media coverage— newspaper, radio, and a TV program called *There Is a Way*.

I was very fortunate to become one of seven interfaith religious speakers in a large Catholic church, where about three hundred religious leaders of different faiths were part of about a thousand people, all celebrating the memory of the late Doctor Martin Luther King, Jr. I'd known only about a week before that I was going to be one of the speakers, and I'd given a lot of thought as to my subject, but it kept eluding me. I should mention here that I do not write my talks or speak very well if I use notes; it just comes out stilted, so I don't do that. What I usually do is think about a subject and then let it flow naturally. Despite my attempts, I could not come up with what felt right. When I got onto the stage, I still hadn't a clue what I was going to speak about. I was about the fifth speaker to talk.

The first speaker was a Rabbi who spoke beautifully, eloquently, and brilliantly. The second speaker, a young black minister, spoke fantastically and flawlessly for about fifteen minutes and was the only one to get a standing ovation for his incredible talk. The next two speakers spoke well and efficiently. Just before the fifth speaker, also a Rabbi, got up, I said a silent, brief prayer. Addressing my Spiritual Self, I said, "If I ever needed your help, I need it now. These people are professionals doing a fabulous job. I'm not only outleagued, I haven't even chosen a subject. I don't know what I'm to say."

Suddenly, the Rabbi was seated, and I was at the podium, and from my talk, people had to realize that I was spontaneous. I didn't recall the details of what I said, but the essence was that I praised what the other speakers had shared, and asked the congregation to not so much hear the words as to feel them in their hearts. I shared that I was speaking from my heart to their hearts, and that we needed to *be* the peace we talk about, and come more from our hearts than from our heads. I did not receive a standing ovation, but as usual, the Universal Power came through and was there for me, and it was good.

I then managed to get a ride to San Diego. You can't walk to it from Los Angeles because the route is mainly freeways. I spoke to a group called the TELEOS Institute and was written up in their magazine. I also had articles in the *San Diego Province* and *Sun* newspapers, as well as radio bleeps. I suffered from minor back problems before and during my walk, but, even so, while my hosts were out I thought I would surprise them and vacuum. Well, I shouldn't have done that! I must have twisted and really put my back out. Friends returning to Los Angeles took me back there and I saw a chiropractor who helped straighten me out, somewhat.

I heard that there was a walk of global walkers, 150 of them, "Global Walkers for a Livable World," leaving Santa Monica, California on February 1, 1990 for New York, as the first of three phases circling the globe. I arranged to walk with them on the first day, and said that I was also headed for New York. I would meet up with them periodically as we crisscrossed the country. Meanwhile, I arranged to ride out to visit The Friends of Peace Pilgrim, in Hemet, California. They were very gracious hosts to me for nearly a week. We got to know one another and are now friends. I try to contact them about once a month to let them know what's going on and to get their news. They are set up to distribute the books and tapes they've made of the original Peace Pilgrim. As already mentioned, after my visit in Hemet, I rode back to Los Angeles to join the Global Walkers.

CHAPTER FIVE

Joining the Global Walkers for a Livable World

FEBRUARY 1, 1990 was a beautiful day in Santa Monica, California, as hundreds of people gathered there at the beach to be part of a ritual for the commencement of the "Global Walk for a Livable World." The mayor of Santa Monica wished us well, as did some of the movie stars joining the occasion. Some of the walkers went into the Pacific Ocean, knowing that their next ocean swim would be at the Atlantic on the East Coast. By about noon the walk got underway. We stopped off at a church for a brief ceremony and received blessings for a safe and successful journey. I left the group when we got to Westwood, their first night's destination, and I stayed in Los Angeles for five more days. Then I left to follow them on foot to New York and to meet up with them occasionally, as earlier stated.

I'd walked about ten miles through the San Fernando Valley, which is all built up, and I was trying to decide where I might sleep that night, when a car pulled up at a traffic signal, and the driver yelled, "Meet me around the corner; I want to talk to you." So I walked round the corner where he'd parked, wondering what this experience was going to bring. I was delighted, but not surprised. He lived about two blocks away and was inviting me for food and maybe accommodations, if his wife was in agreement. When I arrived at their home, they spread out the red carpet for me, not literally, but they couldn't have been more gracious. Strangers one moment, friends the next. Life is fun. No wonder I enjoy my *Work,* or should I say *Life,* for I enjoy what I am doing.

Next day, I walked to Burbank, and decided I'd sleep at the airport waiting room, but at about 10:30 P.M., I learned that they close the airport at 11 P.M., so I'd have to leave. For where? I didn't like calling friends that late at night, but I did call, and they drove down five miles to pick me up, and I ended up sleeping in a bed. I continued the next day, and gave a surprise talk at one of the churches, where I was immediately invited for food and accommodations that night. I became a guest of the Santa Ana Church. Not only was I accommodated and fed, but they kindly volunteered to print a newsletter for me. This is the way life can be and needs to be—everyone helping each other to help each other. I wandered into Claremont, east of Los Angeles, and stopped to talk with a man who was gardening and who seemed to want a break. We talked for about an hour, and he mentioned that the Global Walkers had gone by two days ago.

I had felt bad about making arrangements to see them, for as I left Los Angeles, I realized that, as they had backup busses, they must have been a hundred miles ahead of me, and there was no way I could catch up as promised, especially as I made stops along the way and gave talks. Nevertheless, I was encouraged by this news and decided to hitchhike, even though I don't like doing that. So I spent the day walking about ten miles while getting three rides, to do a total of thirty miles. I met up with them in the late afternoon, just as they were camping for the night in Joshua Tree, California. I told them that I'd walk with them the next day, but that I would leave and make no promises to see them again, as they probably would be moving too fast. They asked me to stay on and walk with them, but I said that as Peace Pilgrim usually walked alone, I too would walk alone. Also, I didn't have a penny to contribute towards the walk anyway, and I knew that they were requiring $3,000 for food and gas from the walkers for their nine month walk. They said, "You don't understand; we're offering you a scholarship." I decided that I could walk with them for a while, and that I would have plenty of time to walk alone again afterwards. So, I graciously accepted their generous offer.

Dawn broke the next morning, and after we were fed, me included, we broke up camp and resumed walking. We'd walked for about thirty minutes and, suddenly, we were in the desert, and it went on and on and on, as far as the eye could see. And that was just the beginning. I felt suddenly very relieved and emotional as I thought of how my Spiritual Power had again come through, without my even asking, to bring me the support I required. How could I possibly have thought that, without a penny in my pocket and only a half-pint bottle of water, I could walk hundreds of miles across the deserts, but being unfamiliar with deserts, I'd just blindly trusted that it would work out, and as always, it did!

Soon after we'd started into the California desert, we came across hundreds of windmills rotating at full blast, generating enough electricity for the city of Palm Springs and vicinities. Being an ecological group, we were very pleased to see this use of alternative energy. In fact, we set up a fan on our refrigerator truck to generate electricity for use when we were parked. We also used portable solar panels to provide electricity for our mobile office equipment and other electrical needs, such as keeping our batteries charged.

I enjoyed many conversations along the walk, though often, for safety reasons, we'd walk alone, in single file, to contemplate, take in the desert scenery, or just plain walk, covering the California, Arizona, and New Mexico deserts, and then the Texas Panhandle, which was like a desert as far as I was concerned, with strong winds blowing sand that got into everything, including our meals and our mouths, not to mention the zip fasteners on my tent. Finally, we all got to Oklahoma, which had trees, hills, and farm country.

Walking and living with a large group of people was a new experience for me. The group was about as diversified as they come, with young people and older people from all parts of the financial, educational, social, and cleanliness spectra. I got plenty of opportunity to walk my talk to be at peace. It was a great learning experience, and I was surprised to realize that I was somewhat of a snob, with some biases that I was unaware I had. As the walk proceeded, I was struck that some of "those," who I had judgmentally labeled in my mind, turned out to be super people, and I'm grateful for these lessons. Some others I found I could love, but not like or accept their behavior. And that was okay, for I wished them well without choosing to be with them.

Included in our walk were people from other countries—Dutch, Germans, Spanish, and half a dozen people from the former Soviet Union. Fortunately, most of the group spoke at least some English, so language wasn't a problem or a barrier, and we were able to communicate. However, to get the picture, one has to realize that we were 150 spirited, independent thinking, noncompliant people. Yet, through conflict resolution and consensus group thinking, we were able to meet, walk, and move our travelling city, with all that that entails—obtaining food and water, cooking, doing dishes, making toilet disposal arrangements, dealing with bus breakdowns and blistered feet—and still survive! We were there for one another, and friendships, marriages, and divorces were all part of it.

Let me just digress for a moment to say how much our society needs to catch up with learning to live and care about each other. I'd not thought of this, but somewhere it was pointed out to me that many people join the military, with all that that may entail, because they want to feel cared for by somebody, and they know that their buddies are prepared to risk their lives for them. This is undoubtedly true of gangs, too. Isn't it a sad reflection on society that we are prepared to criticize only, but are not prepared to be there for one another. The time to care for one another is now, my friends. It's long overdue, and too late for some.

We spoke at many schools across the country. I generally stressed the need for and methods of developing a high self-esteem, so that by caring about ourselves, we feel more comfortable about caring for others. Until we've grown sufficiently secure in ourselves, we may tend to seek attention to/for ourselves. Because we may feel rejected, left out, or not cared for, we try to obtain attention using unacceptable behavior, which, though it does bring focus, is self-defeating. As we grow secure, we feel less threatened, and we begin to include others in our thoughts, and as we do this, we begin to become interested in their welfare, also. With this foundation established, the various other speakers would go on to share the need for ecology, and how each of us can do our part.

I received quite an education in this way on conservation. They taught children a lot of obvious things, such as switching off lights when not required (and to do it, not ignore the importance of it), to wet their toothbrushes and turn off the faucet until ready to rinse, and to encourage washing out reusable mugs rather than using non-biodegradable styrofoam cups. They also taught some not-so-obvious things like, if Americans would consume only ten percent less meat per week, we could save the forests presently being cut down to provide more grain for cattle. We could feed the hungry by supplying them the grain instead of squandering the large quantities required by cattle. Then we could conserve both rain forests and the enormous amount of water required to grow all those grains.

Many of the children were already well informed, and we encouraged them to have the adults at home join them in recycling. I think that we made great headway across the country on Earth Day, with people taking notice. Yet, we've a long way to go to get governments to efficiently deal with these problems instead of creating them with nuclear testing, bombing, oil wells, ocean oil pollution, as well as all the other pollution dumped into the sea and atmosphere, not to mention the hazards of nuclear waste that will be around for thousands of years while we tenaciously continue to mine the same raw materials that we don't even yet know how to dispose of.

There's no question in my mind that love is the only solution to all of our problems, so we'd better take notice, or perish. Love is caring about each other, and it starts with me. Love is also being alert to what's going on and having the courage and using the energy that it takes to right these wrongs for the benefit of all, and not just for the few. To be blissful, spiritual, and peaceful does not mean sitting on the sidelines, watching the world go by. On the contrary, it means being fully alive and fully alert, making the necessary changes in a nonviolent manner. Powerfully, gently, peacefully, and firmly treating others as we want to be treated, but making the necessary changes by taking charge of our own lives and not allowing ourselves to be victims of anyone, we can do it. Indeed, we have to do it if we are to continue to survive.

CHAPTER SIX

Return to Oregon

WITH THE HELP OF CHIROPRACTORS, I'd been able to walk about twenty miles a day, but suddenly, almost overnight, I found myself in great pain trying to cover only two miles. This time, it was not only my back that was troubling me, but my hips, and I knew that I could not continue on to New York as I had planned. Because I had given up everything I'd owned, I had no money or medical insurance, so I decided that as soon as possible, I'd return to Oregon, where I'd be close to family and friends and could wait a year for my Medicare to come due. But first, I proceeded to Tulsa to do a TV news program there, to speak at a Catholic church and at a synagogue before getting a ride with a Unitarian minister to Milwaukee, where I visited the annual Unitarian meeting of ministers and delegates from all over the U.S.A.

A couple at that meeting were heading for St. Paul, Minnesota, and when they heard I was heading for a large meeting in Duluth, they invited me along. They would not hear of my sleeping in the car, but instead fed me and provided me with a motel room. We got to know one another very well on that journey and became a "mutual admiration society" of our own. They were turning in their car rental at the airport at St. Paul, Minnesota, where friends were picking them up. I expressed my gratitude to them for all they had done to enhance my journey and make it possible for me to get to the Duluth meeting in time, and I had some difficulty in persuading them that I'd be okay in finding my way to Duluth. They almost felt guilty for not taking me there, but I told them that I was used to getting from here to there, and it was my mission, so with much concern they finally let me go.

It was now about 11:00 A.M. I had no idea how far from the airport or in which direction the Twin Cities were, so I started making inquiries. I was able to use a courtesy telephone at the airport to try to contact churches and schools, but the best I could come up with was a Jewish agency that would provide me with money. However, because I didn't accept money, their generous offer didn't help me.

By now it was about 1:00 in the afternoon, so I decided that I'd have to just find my way into town. I spoke to one of the hotel shuttle drivers and asked if he could take me part of the way and head me in the direction of town. Although the shuttle was meant only for hotel guests, he did drive me about four miles and set me in the right direction. I hobbled towards town and got to the Salvation Army, which had some bread for the needy, and by then I qualified, so I ate my fill and continued on, as I knew it would be dark in a couple of hours and I had been told that the area was unsafe at night.

I'm not unduly concerned for my safety, but I don't invite problems either, so I was hoping to get a place to sleep. I saw a hospital and thought perhaps, if I contacted the chaplain, I could sleep in his office that night. I did contact the chaplain. Although he wanted to help me, it was against hospital rules for him to do so. He made several calls though, and made arrangements for me at a mission-type sleeping place. I walked about half a mile to it, but when I got there they told me they were full. I did not have the name of the person he'd spoken to, but was assured there was no space available. There was still about forty-five minutes before dark. The sky was very black, and rain was about to fall out of that sky in buckets at any moment.

I found myself another hospital, where I figured I'd contact the chaplain, for some help in calling places, because without money, it's difficult even to make these local calls. Unfortunately, he was in a meeting with family members of a patient and would be with them for some time. The head nurse, however, referred me to the YMCA, about a half mile away. When I left the hospital to go there, the rain was coming down heavily, so I arrived very wet, hungry, and tired at about 8:30 P.M. I'd been up from about seven that morning. Fortunately, I'd slept wonderfully in the motel, but it had been a long day, and I was ready to sleep. The YMCA, unfortunately, was no longer one with accommodations. It just had swimming and gym facilities. I'd drawn a blank.

The receptionist offered to help me, called a Union Mission, and arranged for me to be there that night, so I had a place to stay, but she said it was five miles away. I indicated that probably was more than I could handle that night, thanked her, and said I'd manage it somehow. She then said that if I'd wait an hour for her to finish work, she'd drop me off, as it was on her way home. With much appreciation, I accepted the offer.

Actually, when she dropped me off, it had seemed more like a mile than five, but I was thrilled to be there. I was admitted into a room with about forty men and designated a bunk bed. The sheets were clean, and I was asleep in minutes, before the lights were turned out. When I awoke, I was delighted to find that they had a shower and hot water. As I thought about it, I was reminded of my service in the Royal Air Force, where we'd also had about forty men to a billet, but I'd never expected to experience that situation again and be grateful for the opportunity. I was provided with breakfast and left the mission much more comfortably than when I'd arrived.

I returned to the hospital to complete arrangements with the head nurse, who'd accepted my offer to speak at the staff, doctors', and nurses' meeting. She was going to put out a flyer, and I was to speak there the next day. The storm had cleared, so I walked into the city and was directed to a Dorothy Day Center, where I was able to get a meal and, while I lined up to do so, met a husband and wife who were volunteers there. They invited me to their home, where I spent a very pleasant evening with their family. I spent the night there also, and the next day was driven to the hospital where I gave the talk. I told them that I was headed for a Rainbow Gathering of several thousand people about ninety miles from Duluth. One of the nurses was heading for Duluth and gave me a ride.

When I arrived in Duluth, it was the day before the meeting was to start. I decided to begin walking, in the hopes that I'd be recognized and offered a ride. I hobbled about two miles when I saw a bus filled with people stopped at a service station for gas, and some of them were in its store buying munchies. I inquired if they were headed for the meeting and was greeted with "YES, hop in and join us." This felt really good, even though when we set off, we were packed to capacity. I'd never been to this group's gathering before, and had tentatively thought of giving a talk or offering a workshop if it fit into their plans, but when I got there, I realized that it was like eight campgrounds, with people visiting each other, relaxing, cooking, swimming, looking after the children, and having a sort of weekend market of wares.

One area had drumming that lasted all through the night. This was all a new experience for me. I offered a meditation for those interested, and mainly mingled or spoke on a one-to-one basis wherever I happened to be. They were friendly, caring, and concerned people, all enjoying one another and nature's beauty in outdoor living. It was nice to see so many people in harmony together in this down-to-earth setting, and I appreciated the expo-sure to people from all over the U.S.A. who'd gathered for this meeting. I made it known that I required a ride to the west coast and accepted one in a van with six other people. They squeezed me in and I felt fortunate, as they were heading to Eureka, California. However, it turned out to be a grueling and harrowing experience. Most of the passengers had paid some of the fare for the journey, and I'd offered to do extra turns in driving if that would be acceptable. What I did not know before we were on the road was that the vehicle was not roadworthy. It looked okay, but the steering was worn out, and one needed to turn the steering wheel what seemed like a quarter of a turn before it would respond, so that we were constantly compensating, trying to keep it driving straight, and since we were driving at the speed limit, it was quite a responsibility with so many people on board.

I usually treat problems as opportunities in disguise, but I had to stretch in this case, for I had two other concerns. One, I was by far the oldest, in a group that enjoyed modern music turned up to full volume. And two, I was without food, so that when at night we stopped at a rest stop that offered complementary coffee and two danish, I partook of both. I ordinarily do not drink coffee, but I was thirsty, and since I was doing so much driving, I thought it would help to keep me awake. The combination of the coffee and the very sweet danish on an empty stomach was too much, and after a few more miles of driving, I had to pull off the road and was violently ill. Someone else had to drive, and I sat/lay in the bumpy vehicle, concerned that I felt too awful to carry out my obligation of driving, and not knowing what other compensation to offer instead. I must have dropped off to sleep for a few hours, for when I awoke the day was dawning, and I felt okay enough to drive again, and fortunately I did not feel that I could eat anything, so not having food was not a problem for me. By the time we reached California, I was feeling better, and one of the passengers offered me a sandwich.

By now I was getting used to taking rides. I do not like setting an example of hitchhiking, but sometimes I found it absolutely necessary. I got to Newport to visit a chiropractic friend, who helped my physical condition considerably. I was invited to stay with friends in nearby Lincoln City, for months if necessary, so that I could attend the three times a week treatment that my chiropractic friend provided for me as a charity, which he preferred to call his opportunity to help keep me going on my mission. I knew that I had a physical problem that was getting relief from the treatment, but it was still keeping me from being able to walk any distance, and it was thought that I had worn out a hip.

I believe in the maxim, "Physician, heal thyself," so I turned it over to my Spiritual Nature, fully expecting a miraculous healing. I believe that when we turn our problems over to the universe, we still need to do what we can to help the situation, but that we can do it in a trusting, relaxed, preferential manner, expecting a miracle and allowing to have happen what happens, and not with a demand, which, if that exact thing is not forthcoming, sets us up for disappointment. I believe, know, and trust that the Spiritual Self knows best, and I'm accepting of whatever consequences occur. However, doing my part, I read a book called *Somatics*. It's a reawakening of the mind's control of movement, flexibility, and health, by Thomas Hanna, director of the Novato Institute for Somatic Research and Training. I was extremely impressed by its contents and decided to write Thomas Hanna for an appointment. Nearly three weeks went by and I hadn't a reply, but friends travelling to California offered to drop me off at Novato, so I went with them.

They let me off at his office and continued on to their destination. I found the office closed, and upon inquiring discovered that Mister Hanna had been killed in a car accident two weeks earlier. Since I did not have an appointment, I'd been somewhat prepared that I might not see him, but his death came as a shock to me. I discovered that Doctor Jim Dreaver, Chiropractor, of nearby Sebastopol, had trained under Thomas Hanna and was practicing his treatments, and he was prepared to see me and to squeeze me into his very busy schedule. Not only did he see me, but he insisted on seeing me the following day also, to relieve some of the pain before I returned north to Lincoln City.

I again found it necessary to hitchhike, usually without incident, but just outside of Crescent City, California, a small truck stopped for me. A passenger got out and invited me into the front between himself and the driver. I sat down. I was sandwiched in the middle, and almost before starting off he said that they needed money for gas. I explained that as Peace Pilgrim II, I had no money, but that I'd gladly get out to make room for someone else who could perhaps help pay for gas, but they didn't want to do that. So I was stuck in the middle on a journey that I'd rather not have taken—especially as a few miles on, I realized that they were on drugs. Our driver passed a car with an oncoming car approaching. We barely missed them, and he turned to me and said, "That scared you, didn't it?" Under the circumstances, I felt little option but to humor him and hope that he wouldn't repeat such a performance again. I was more than prepared to leave them early, but I'd already told them that I was heading further north, so they took me to their destination, Gold Beach. I was not anxious to continue hitchhiking, but my Universal Power took care of me, and I arrived back in Lincoln City in one piece!

The chiropractic treatments were very helpful, but I knew that I could no longer continue my mission on foot. The original Peace Pilgrim had decided on her mission and walked the country for twenty-eight years without becoming sick once during all that time. I had not wanted to be Peace Pilgrim, had fought the idea for ten days and nights, and when I decided to accept this assignment I had already been having chiropractic treatment and required increasing amounts of it throughout my walk. I figured that eventually I'd discover the reason why all this was happening, and I needed, again, to put my trust in my Spiritual Power.

As I reflected on the situation, I decided that this would be the right time to write my book, so that's what I started to do. I came to the conclusion that perhaps it was time to give up being Peace Pilgrim II and return to start a new life, but that didn't feel right, and I felt that I wanted to continue on, if possible, being Peace Pilgrim II. I decided to let it be known that I needed a vehicle to be donated if I was to remain travelling; meanwhile, I would stay put, writing, basically letting the Spiritual Nature make the decisions.

About six weeks later, I got a call from a friend who'd heard through the grapevine that I needed a vehicle, and he was donating one. I'd already realized that a vehicle is an expense, with gas, insurance, and repairs, and that I'd no longer be able to function without money. I knew that I was eligible for Social Security, and so I made the decision that I would draw upon it and rely upon speaking engagements, honorariums, workshops, and love offerings to support my vehicle and myself, and that I would make a start from the beginning again to mainly support myself. I feel the message of peace is what's important, and not the means of transportation, and that having a car will be more efficient, enabling me to travel greater distances in less time, so as to give more talks and reach more people.

CHAPTER SEVEN

Continuing the Journey

IT WAS THE BEGINNING of January, 1991, when I went to Eugene to pick up my car. I expected to be gone for just a few days, to return to Lincoln City for a couple more weeks to do more writing, and to organize an itinerary to continue on the road. However, the news was highlighting the probability of war with Iraq, and I felt the need to, in some way, help prevent that from happening.

When I arrived in Eugene, I started organizing a protest rally. The media had wanted to interview me as Peace Pilgrim II, so I asked them to do so at the rally, which would give them additional news and also highlight our desire for peace through conflict resolution rather than force. Fortunately, they agreed.

As soon as the rally was over, I was able to drive to Portland and be part of a massive protest rally there. Then it was on to Seattle, Washington, for yet another protest march, after which, I headed on to Vancouver, British Columbia for a final one. I really appreciated having the car just in time to make this possible. In Vancouver, I also participated in a large Dr. Martin Luther King Anniversary Parade, and finally gave in to the fact that I could no longer physically hobble on in any more marches, yet the work has to go on, and it does.

I have to admit that it is completely beyond my understanding that there are still so many people who consider war to be fun because of the camaraderie and excitement that it seems to bring to their life. Their talking about war games tells us something. Considering the wounded victims, widows, and parents of the deceased, the misery of hundreds of thousands of refugees, the destruction,

41

and all the vile consequences of war, both physical and mental, how can some, because of power or financial greed, still endorse such hell?

It is my feeling that the most important priority of each and every one of us who is still sane, should be to seek peace, in every way that we can. Our priorities need to be focused on learning to live in harmony and avoiding the pitfalls of power and greed. Fortunately, science is beginning to prove from the experience with atoms, neutrons, electrons, protons, and quantum physics theories, that everything is interconnected. Many of us are already aware that what affects others, eventually affects us. We need to become compassionate and concerned, to stand up and do something constructive, to change our priorities from munitions to the homeless, the hungry, the sick, and the aged. With income taxes misdirected to military purposes, there's not enough funding to keep mentally sick people taken care of, so that they are out wandering in the streets, till they are caught murdering or raping someone. Then, somehow, there's funding made available to get them put in jail and to support them there. To turn this situation around, we have to get our thinking and our priorities right, or suffer the ever increasing consequences. When will we learn? Surely now is the time.

I was relieved that the Israelis had the restraint not to enter the Gulf War. Had they done so, I feel that it may have become a global conflict. As it was, the tragedy, though short lived as a war, was horrendous both to the enemy and on world ecology. It still lingers on, and to what end? How could some in the U.S.A. celebrate a victory, after all the butchery and savagery of war? The Iraqi leader still remains in command, which is another thing I can't fathom. The only blessing I saw in the whole picture was the relatively few American casualties, and those were mainly caused by "friendly fire"! How can we buy into such deceptive wording? All wars are bloody, horrible, and losers. I was glad when it was over to return to sharing my messages. I am for peace in our hearts, which then extends out to others, so that all these barbaric, outmoded practices will come to belong to the past, so that the kind of world that we really want will finally become a reality.

Here are a few ideas that I believe can help this process to happen. I believe that we each need to be aware that "Peace begins with me." How we behave, each one of us, does make a difference, and our attitudes and behavior create a reaction from others. Therefore one must continually ask, "Am I projecting peace and a constructive approach to life, or am I perpetuating war, through negativity, low self-esteem, hostility, and force?" I feel that what the world needs is a massive, mature education. It is my ardent hope that this book will be a help in that direction. Money needs to be spent by Madison Avenue, the advertising media, to promote the workable principles of the Golden Rule—understanding, caring, and compassion. This should become the New American Way. I'm thrilled that many schools have started to teach conflict resolution. Perhaps we adults can learn it from the children, from the mouths of babes, as it were.

Though normal education is important, I feel it is essential that we first need to be in harmony with the principles of life that work, so that we discover how to live in harmony with our relations and strangers. As we come to care about others, we will heal our planet and restore it to sanity. I believe that through the fast moving changes that have occurred, we have become apathetically numbed, and have allowed our government, in the guise of patriotism, to go to war, and even now to spend billions on unneeded ammunitions and billions more of our money on many scandals, such as the savings and loan bailout. It seems that we're finally awakening, and we're replacing our apathy with anger and distrust of what we have allowed to happen. I hope that the action we take to remedy this absurd situation will be powerful, and most important, peaceful. If we want peace, we have to demonstrate peace in our actions.

There is need here for great strength of purpose, for brilliant minds with caring hearts to turn their attention from the greedy to the needy, from dishonesty to good, old-fashioned principles of trust, honesty, integrity, and concern for the people. It is a step in the right direction that we know the principle of the Golden Rule, and that *love overcomes hatred, and the value of being honest and truthful.* These are all love skills that have been talked about for eons, but nothing will change until we each take responsibility to live them. The adage that "deeds speak louder than words" was never truer than it is in this case. What could be more important than love and peace? It needs to become our top privilege and priority, individually and collectively. I'm sure that when we reach the shores of the pearly gates, that the question asked will not be, "How much material have you gained," but rather "How much have you loved and contributed?"

About May, 1991, I returned to Eugene to stay with some friends, Bill and Shakti Wilson and their sons. While there, I gave some local talks and investigated some alternative healing processes for my hips. I was invited to join a delegation going to Israel to dialogue between the Israelis and the Palestinians. I became part of that dialogue and spent almost the entire month of June there. We stayed at the Notre Dame Hotel. It was opposite Damascus Gate in Jerusalem on the Green Line, which is a dividing line between the Israeli and Palestinian sections of the city. We travelled quite extensively there, seeing the plight of the Palestinian refugees and hearing of their hardships. Also, we spoke with many Israelis. It was difficult to learn the depths of the problem there, and I found my mind like a windshield wiper, feeling empathy first for the one side, and then feeling the understanding and the fears of the other. The culture there is so different from that of the U.S.A. I'm glad that our mission was not to judge the differences, but rather to encourage dialogue and peace in whatever ways we could. I feel that we made friends with both sides, and that perhaps in our own way we were able to add a touch of bonding cement here and there.

When we returned to the U.S.A., I was invited by one of the delegates to stay in California. My hips seemed to be deteriorating, and I was considering an offer of remaining in Orange County and working in that area, which had lots of opportunity that entailed only local travel. However, I had previously made a commitment that I would speak at the Annual Unity Western Region Retreat in Washington State, so I left Orange County heading north to honor that agreement. On my way, I stopped off at Asilomar for about a week at the Annual Religious Science Church Retreat and had the privilege of addressing one of the classes there. Asilomar is a beautiful location near Monterey, and I very much enjoyed my stay with this group of enthusiastic, positive people.

I drove through some incredible scenery in Washington State to the Unity Retreat near Mount Rainier. This meeting was also full of enthusiastic people, which helps one to reestablish faith in humanity. I keep being reminded how precious people are, particularly as they become aware of using their talents and skills in caring, constructive ways.

Being so close to the Canadian border, I planned on visiting my son and family, who live about forty miles east of Vancouver, British Columbia. I intended to stay for a few days; however, I was invited to attend the planetary session of the Interfaith Network up there, an annual event that this year would be held in Vancouver. I travelled into Vancouver and accepted the hospitality of my various hosts for accommodations for a couple of weeks, and gave TV and radio interviews while waiting for the meeting date to arrive. I'm glad I was exposed to and participated with this North American Interfaith group. I feel very blessed in my work for peace, and for the exposure I get to see so many people involved in improving our planet.

By now the condition of my hips had worsened to where my son had to help me walk down the stairs, and I was acting and beginning to feel like I was eighty years old, unable to stand for any length of time and hardly able to walk. I decided that the quality of my life and work were beginning to suffer, so I'd need to return to Eugene to explore a couple more alternative healing methods. Chiropractors, masseurs, and others worked on me, and I could see that I would have to be in Eugene for a long session of treatments, and would therefore have to stretch my Social Security to include renting an unfurnished room in somebody's house. Friends helped me with some furniture, and I became comfortably settled, making Eugene my headquarters and driving locally in Oregon to meetings and lecturing appointments.

For about nine months I stayed with these various treatments, convinced that I would receive a miraculous healing, but it became obvious that I was to be healed through surgery. I did have my hip

replaced. Twenty-two years ago, this would not have been possible
in the U.S.A., but now through modern technology, the miracle of
this surgery is changing my life to where I'm beginning to feel more
like a 45-year-old. Not bad, going from 66 to 80 to 45, all in one year's
span. Ha! Although now I'm healing and doing great, I'm not quite
out of the woods. X-rays show that the other hip has deteriorated to
where it, too, needs replacing.

I had, during this time, teamed up with a professional video
man, who volunteered to make video tapes of my being interviewed
and speaking at schools in Eugene and nearby Corvallis. Unfortunately, these were not edited, but became an addition to my portfolio
that may be available in the future. I also spent time getting this book
together for publication. At the time it was just before the 1992
Presidential election, and I hoped that Bill Clinton and Senator Gore
would make it to the top. I felt very confident that if they did, their
new, young leadership would inspire the world, as Kennedy did,
and help us in our breakthrough towards a new utopian era.

It's true that the world faces many problems, but it is also true that
there are many individuals and groups who have a vision of a more
harmonious way of life, and they are doing something about it. If you
feel that you'd like to be counted as well, just check out who's doing
what in your area, and I encourage you to get involved. The more of
us who get involved, the sooner we'll turn the world around. As you
already know, I'm an ardent believer that "Peace begins with me,"
and that that's the most important starting point. By getting ourselves
in harmony within all aspects of our own lives, we become more in
tune with ourselves and find that we're not in competition, but in
cooperation with like groups. We rise beyond our particular group
to include others who seek peace in the unity of our diversity, to form
an harmonious, living symphony. As and when our thinking, feeling,
and action express this contentment and appreciation of our Spiritual
Power, the transformation takes place. It's happening throughout the
world in individuals, and in ones and twos, small groups, and festival
gatherings. Unlike the 1960s, the roots are now deeply planted. Wise
men and women are now networking the new world to replace a
crumbling old one. Let us approach the new century with goodwill

towards all humankind, as a reality, by seeking to express our highest potential in our daily lives.

The day after the Presidential elections, I was thrilled and delighted to see that Governor Clinton, now President Elect Clinton, and his cohort, Senator Gore, had made it, and would soon be President and Vice President, respectively, of this great country, and I felt that, for the first time in ages, we had the opportunity to really begin to start working towards peace and towards the needs, rather than the greeds, of one another. I still feel this window of opportunity, which has the power to work, by example, right from the top down. Each one of us can jump aboard at any time, because we are prepared and ready to join in a healing of the planet. It begins with me as an individual.

On August 25, 1992, I had surgery to replace my left hip, after which complications set in, shutting down my bladder, so that in September I had to have prostate surgery.

My new hip felt so good that I decided not to wait to have the other one replaced. So, in January, 1993, I had surgery to replace my right hip. While it was still healing, I discovered that I had cancer of the colon, and so in March I had surgery to remove the cancered portion of the colon. It appears that they removed all of the cancer and the prognosis is very good. I'm healing well and am daily gaining back my strength.

In between surgeries, I was able to give talks and workshops fairly locally, and for the rest of the year I planned to work mainly in the Northwestern States, as well as to attend the 1993 Council for a Parliament of World Religions Centennial Meeting at Chicago in August/September of that year.

Some of you may feel that this must have been a terrible time for me, and I admit that it was not pleasant; however I give thanks that the magic of modern surgery has given me the opportunity to regain my health and become young again. I feel fortunate to have had proper medical care, but my heart goes out to those in embattled countries whose suffering has been so much worse and often untreated. I am truly grateful for my blessings. Thank you, my Eternal Spirit of God.

SECTION TWO
Towards Understanding

CHAPTER EIGHT

Understanding

TOWARDS UNDERSTANDING

I'D LIKE TO SHARE some of my beliefs with you:

I believe that peace begins with me.

I believe that I'm responsible for my actions and behavior.

I believe in letting go of blame, by viewing individuals as distinct from their actions. One is then able, rather than condemning them, to encourage them to their highest potential.

I believe in treating others as I want them to treat me.

I believe that love overcomes hatred.

I believe in forgiveness of myself and of others.

I believe in having a high self-esteem.

I believe in conflict resolution rather than force.

I believe in living unconditional love.

I believe that we are unique, precious, and more than just okay.

I believe that the Spirit of the Universal power is within me/us, and I believe in Its empowerment.

I believe that all things are possible.

I believe that we have incredible potential and enormous Inner Power.

I believe in gratitude and appreciation of Nature's every gift, the flowers, trees, people, and animals.

I believe that our thoughts become our actions. I believe that we have choices.

I believe in high principles of honesty, integrity, responsibility, consideration, compassion, and fairness.

I believe in being assertive, and that gentleness is a strength, not a weakness.

I believe that we are privileged as parents to help develop the awareness of our Universal Power in our children.

If you or your group are in agreement with the above, you might want to make copies of it and sign them as personal commitments for yourselves.

SUGGESTIONS

This second section of the book is written in essay form. You might wish to ponder, contemplate, or meditate on each essay's content before proceeding to the next chapterette. I have written from my heart to yours, so that the words may go deeper than surface level. If you resonate with these messages and wish to perpetuate love into the world, I invite you to use this section as a manual. I suggest that you gather a group of friends together; they can be acquaintances from clubs, business, church, gymnasium, peace groups, or other organizations, and create a Big Talk (rather than a small talk) group.

You could read a chapter, take a few minutes of silence to let it penetrate, then discuss how you feel about it, weighing the pros and cons, sharing how it relates to you, and/or adding your own views. You might meet each week with a different chapterette for your discussion group, and should you do this, I would suggest a few guidelines. The first would be that this is for your personal growth, not to prove yourself right. You may find yourselves having many differing opinions, and a benefit here is to learn how to disagree without being disagreeable. This is best done by supporting one another without put-downs. Discern, but do not judge one another. Be there for each other and for your mutual growth. You will soon discover that you have created an extended family of caring, trusting friends. You may even wish to start an additional group with other friends.

It's exciting to think how this might expand and help turn the world away from fear toward love and self-esteem. Should you wish to use any part of this book as articles for your church or other groups' publications, or as letters to the editor, or to your local newspaper, city official, or your congressperson, by all means do so. Whatever you can do to help spread the word is much appreciated. In fact, should your group develop helpful ideas on the subjects we've covered, you might choose to send them in as weekly/ monthly articles to your local newspaper, to help your community learn alternative ways of handling life. I'd appreciate your sending me a copy, too, that I might create a radio program around your ideas and further spread the message.

Conflict Resolution

Conflict resolution uses discernment, not judgment. Compare the old way of settling differences, then use the conflict resolution method, and see which you think would be best for you. Consider the following example:

Two good people care about one another, and all is going well. The couple has worked all week. The weather is beautiful, and it is now the weekend, an opportunity to enjoy catching up on projects, hobbies, visiting friends, travelling, or whatever. Then a learning situation presents itself. A difference of opinion occurs, resulting in personal blame:

Wife: We need to do chores, and get things done, but you *never* want to do them. You *always* want to go out and avoid these responsibilities.

Husband: What's wrong with going out on weekends? You *always* want us to stay home and work.

Blame causes friction, so they are off on a collision course of either defensiveness or aggressiveness for each to try and prove that they're right. The husband may stay and do the chores, but he feels resentful. Meanwhile the wife may be happy that the chores are being done, but she may be upset because of the resentment. What happened to what might otherwise have been a happy day?

The new way might be the Conflict Resolution way. Ask, "What is our problem? I want us to go out. You want us to do the chores. How do we resolve the problem?"

Here are some rules or guidelines to help:

1) I'm okay, you're okay. We just need to resolve our difference of opinion. Focus on the problem that needs to be resolved, and keep personalities out of it.

2) Recognize the need to show each other greater respect.

3) Let's agree to differ, to compromise, to achieve loving results and a win-win game. I'm going to listen, without interrupting, to what it is that you want. What will make you comfortable in this situation? I am going to listen to you, concentrating on what you're telling me. I'm really hearing you, giving you my undivided attention, and not just letting you ramble while I think of what it is that I want to say to win my point. I'm really hearing you, one hundred percent.

When you've finished, I'm going to sum up, or repeat what I've heard you say, and then I'm going to ask, "Is that what you said, and is there anything else?" If there is, I'll again listen, and I'll repeat the sum-up of what it is that I heard you say, and repeat the procedure until you are finished with this issue.

What I have achieved so far is that, I've demonstrated my love and respect for you as a partner. I've demonstrated the Golden Rule.

He or she, the partner, will now know that they'll not only be listened to, but that they'll really be heard and understood. Hopefully, by concentrating on the issues you will not get sidetracked into attacking personalities.

Now it's time for the other partner to do the talking and the second one to do the listening. Using the same format as above, namely, showing respect, really listening, staying noncritical, with the issue, and not attacking the person. When the second partner is completed and satisfied that they have been listened to, heard, and understood, then you are ready to go to the next phase, a win-win situation with no losers or festering resentment. Agree from new, mutual viewpoints as to what the bottom line is, the problem that needs to be resolved. To resolve the problem, you want "this" to happen, so you discuss, "This is what I want." Discuss what you can do to compromise, so that you can each get your own needs met, and then live with the compromise. Perhaps you could try this solution for a month, and another solution for another month, and see how it works out. Then again discuss, for mutual benefit, how to resolve the issue, if it still exists. Remember, this is to be a *win-win* situation, and keep personalities out of it.

In summary, both persons have been respectful, heard each other, cared for each other, resolved at least temporarily an issue that both can live with for awhile, and been fair with each other trying to improve the problem situation. Therefore, you've done the best you can, and even if you've not yet solved the problem, you've improved the relationship by trying to. At worst, you might reach a stalemate wherein you agree to differ, and say, "Well, we can't agree in this case, but I respect your viewpoint, and vice-versa. That way we can still love each other without agreeing on the issue."

What other alternatives are there? You could postpone the solution, each think about alternative solutions, seek more information, study it, and agree to discuss it again in a week. Or you could get outside help, education, or people, such as counselors, and role play the situation. Play with it! This is for your benefit. Learn to have a win-win situation, where each of you ends up being a winner. When one is a loser, there is resentment, and you've both lost.

Understanding More

We once believed that the world was flat, and we once believed that slavery was a way of life. We once believed that war was the answer to aggression. Were we right, or were we wrong? The world is round, slavery is giving way to freedom, and war is no longer an option. Most of us are living stressful lives in a world that has become so complex and frustrating that we look for complex answers that usually just create more problems. What if we could change our world for a better place, with an idea that's so simple that it may at first be scoffed at, just because of its simplicity?

Before you condemn or ignore peace, won't you please give it a try, for your life, and our planet, cannot survive without it. Religions and individuals across the world talk about wanting peace, but we must walk our talk. Peace is more than an absence of war. Because "peace" is not bullying, macho, or manipulating, it is sometimes incorrectly seen as being cowardly, weak, or unpatriotic, but just the opposite is true. It takes courage, strength, conviction, understanding, and self control to offer gentleness and calm in the face of hostility. Jesus, Ghandi, Dr. Martin Luther King and others are adequate proof of this. Peace is innate in all of us. War is taught. We're taught to hate the enemy and to kill in order to survive.

Peace is more than an attitude. It's a skill to be relearned. Peace does not mean just sitting on a log somewhere, meditating. It can, of course, include that, but peace is learning to overcome our fears, because fear is the underlying cause of all of our problems, individually and internationally. Once we overcome our fears, we open ourselves up to trusting and living life fully, comfortably, and joyfully. Madison Avenue, the movie industry, and the media need to get involved to show that peace and love are the simple answer to everything. Our very lives are at stake.

If I loved you, I would not want to wrong or harm you. I'd live the Golden Rule. I'd be a friend to you. I'd listen and really hear what you have to say. Don't we all want to be heard, understood, and respected? Don't we all like to deal with people who are fair, honest, and concerned about us? To have such friends, we need to be such a friend.

If we have a low self-esteem, we feel bad and usually behave accordingly, for we're seeking attention, the wrong kind. With a high self-esteem, we feel good about ourselves and reflect that in our feelings and in our behavior. The obvious solution is to learn to care about ourselves and others.

Practical social solutions for peace might include creating jobs by dismantling all military equipment except for a small amount to be maintained only by the United Nations as a peace force. The military can be put to work rebuilding our nation's bridges, which are disasters waiting to happen, and find other constructive uses. Instead of a Pentagon playing war games, we need to create a Peace Palace of experts in conflict resolution, concentrating on alternative, constructive, national and international nonmilitary products, and ways of teaching and encouraging self-esteem.

I believe that we need a massive, mature education on developing a high self-esteem, and also to promote reviving essential principles, such as speaking the truth, being truthful to ourselves and to others, honesty, integrity, dependability, understanding of conflict resolution, empathy, responsibility, and love. These are the skills that we want and need for joy and survival.

Note that a broad spiritual understanding would encompass all of the above traits. By starting with the premise that we are made in the image and likeness of a Universal Power and that we are the temple housing that Essence, we can then become aware of how spiritually perfect and interconnected we all are. The energy and Universal Power that keeps your heart beating is the same energy that keeps mine beating. However, instead of rejoicing in the inclusiveness, we have sought separation or exclusiveness in specific Gods or religions. I know that *peace begins with me* and that how I behave in my everyday life, particularly with my family, makes a difference.

With a high self-esteem, I live with an attitude of unconditional love, a position that affects everyone I meet peacefully. If, on the other hand, I'm negative, aggressive, and blaming others, because I'm not accepting responsibility for my own behavior, then I am spreading the domino effect of hostility. I have a choice. I can create joy or misery. I personally love, honor, and respect the divinity in everyone, though I don't always agree with their actions or behavior. By discerning rather than judging, I can love the person while totally disagreeing with their actions, and can offer them alternative approaches. This offers constructive help rather than pushing them down.

If people believed in our divinity, we'd treat our children as princes and princesses of the most high, and therefore show them love and consideration, as opposed to the present practices of considering them as an object that we own and may abuse, physically, verbally, psychologically, and sexually. This disgraceful behavior has to stop, and our awareness of our childrens' divinity and preciousness would help that to happen.

We have to become aware of our behavior and learn to forgive ourselves for our mistakes as well as to forgive others for theirs. Forgiving is a freeing experience. Life is full of learning experiences, such as a built-in *guilt* system that's like a red light that says, "Stop!

Look at what you're doing. Don't make that mistake; there's a better way. Go forward constructively with your life." Guilt has then served its purpose and no longer needs to be carried around. As we heed this inner guidance, we begin to see how "Peace begins with me as an individual, and that with my freedom of choice, I can accept responsibility for my life and create unconditional love as the focus for my actions. As an important and precious person who is unique, I am no more and no less important a person than anyone else. I can choose to no longer be a victim by being assertive, not aggressive, and by learning to use conflict resolution to resolve my problems. I will not need to use force, and can use love to overcome hate rather than encouraging hate by hating."

I have outlined what I believe to be constructive options to the problems that we face, so now let's you and I take a look at some of the problems we've created. Although it's not pleasant for us to do so, it's necessary for us to become honest again. Our life-style is built on competition. We've been taught to be first. It doesn't matter who you walk over to get there. Just look at the plight of our homeless, proof of the lack of caring. Steroids are okay, if you don't get caught. So is cheating. Just be number one. We've become greedy and selfish, capable of going into outer space, but unable to get along with our families or our neighbors.

We come from a place of fear—fear of being attacked, fear of losing our jobs, fear of what others may think about us, for we don't feel complete without their approval. There is power and ego, old macho thinking, and bullying, violence, and fighting for what you want. Big business interests are controlling our social interests, and rampant scandal and fraud are everywhere. There is manipulation by advertising and propaganda for blindly loyal flag-waving, to stir up a lynch mob energy into believing that fighting is patriotic: "Go kill the enemy," which we've created by labeling them as evil empires, or as a Hitler. We've believed that conflict resolution is impossible with our enemies.

Our political system, which requires millions of dollars from businesses to elect specific statespersons of their choice for office, also requires looking into. Many of those elected in that way lose their principles, through payback deals on contracts and other scandals. There is the concern of recessing the economy by stopping the military and arms machine. We are feeding war with one billion, nine hundred thousand U.S. dollars, as global companies, each minute of the day and night, produce arms. You don't prepare for peace by creating arms. You end up creating an enemy to justify their manufacture and to test their efficiency.

So, because of wars, look at what we are doing to our world, ecologically, and examine the inhumane ways we are treating one another. At this rate, perhaps we'll have ten more years on this planet before it's too late to make a difference. With a determination and love for peace as a world priority, we can build a paradise like the world has never seen. The choice is ours, and the choice is clear.

Self-Esteem

When you send out love, it tends to come right back to you. There's just an endless supply of it, and all you need to do is keep giving it away. Valentine's Day reminds us of love, so we give gifts to show our love. This is fine, but it's only scraping the surface. We need first to give ourselves love. Have you ever thought of how we beat up on ourselves? Listen to what you are telling yourself. Are you telling yourself how dumb you are for making an error, how no good, how inefficient you are? Most of us do this one way or another, so that we build up an inferiority complex. If someone else criticizes us, it just confirms our mistaken beliefs, so that we feel really sorry for ourselves and give in to feelings of inferiority and inadequacy, or egotistically we fight to prove how great we are on the outside, while lacking self-esteem on the inside.

Lack of self-esteem causes us to drown our pain with alcohol, drugs, and other escapes rather than facing ourselves because of fear of what we may discover: that our life's been one big act. Unless you're a professional or amateur actor, give it up. You can't win playing a false game. Dare to discover that you're not so nice, and you'll discover that you're perfect, beautiful, and pure love. You're a co-creator with the Spiritual Power. As you discover your uniqueness and learn to love yourself, you'll give up guilt and resentment of others.

Self-Esteem (a poem)

You are spiritually perfect
You are not a sinner,
Though you may have sinned
You are not a failure,
Though you may have failed
You are not a success,
Though you may have succeeded
You are not judged,
Though you may have been guilty.

What you are, is . . .

A precious child of the universe,
No more and no less than anyone else.
Whatever you may have done in the yesterday,
Forgive yourself.
One day you will realize that there is not even
Anything to forgive
For the angers and hardships, frustrations and fears,
Have been the very ingredients that have
Spurred you forward to understanding and
Unconditional love.
Yesterday belongs to yesterday,
Tomorrow has not yet arrived.
Delight in today,
Express your love, be joyful, appreciate, and just "be."
You are perfect,
For you are created as, and are part of, the Universal Nature.

The dawning of a day is beautiful, magical and divine. Your personal breakthrough to your Inner Power and perfection is no less spectacular. Let your light shine.

Intuition

The whole of life is one big experience. At a deep level of understanding, there are no rights or wrongs, just experiences from which to learn. We are all at different stages of experience. There is that which is within us . . . intuition if you like . . . that keeps nudging us onward to live in harmony with ourselves, others, and nature. Slowly, we begin to get the message that it's easier to flow with the stream rather than to struggle against it. It's rather like a metaphysical song: "Row, row, row your boat, *gently down* the stream."

A negative person may create a situation or person to blame, and feed the reason with negative energy in the form of bad language, raised voices or shouting, untruths, and even violence. This puts the other person on the offensive or the defensive, thus compounding the problem so that both parties say and do things for which they are later sorry. But in the interim, their frustration may drive them to drink, or, in the case of a marriage, even to other partners.

They may afterwards overcompensate by spoiling themselves or the other person in different ways, such as going out shopping, or buying gifts such as clothes or a new car. This may later be even more frustrating, because the reciprocant may not be wanting a new car in the first place, and now it has to be paid for. Now the first partner may even be angry because they bought the car. So we're off and running again, blaming and justifying our actions, so our prideful nature can be right! There's nothing wrong with buying things, but just examine the motives. Does this all sound familiar? How do we change?

Here are a few suggestions:

Recognize that problems are part of life's experience, giving us the opportunity to solve them and thereby grow. The lessons may be tough, but as we gain strength from them, we begin to recognize that a problem is an opportunity. This helps us to change our attitude to one of acceptance, creating a positive attitude for dealing with it. Don't back away from a problem and try to escape it. Face it and grow. Desire to make a change that will be for the highest good of all concerned. And just do it. Nothing happens till there is action. No mind trips, just action. Do it.

In order to get the right action for right results, we may have to change our thinking, drastically. For much of our lives, we've encountered heavy, locked doors. Here are keys to help open some of them. First, start just where you are. No matter what you've done in the past, forgive yourself, immediately. It's past. It's what you do now that counts. You're okay. Never mind what anyone else says or thinks about you. You're okay. You're a unique creation of the Spiritual Nature. There is no one else in the world exactly like you. Whatever experiences you may have had in the past have been necessary to bring you to this day. Therefore, love yourself, and, from now on, make each day better than yesterday, one day at a time.

You can choose to stop blaming others or judging or justifying. You don't have to prove anything. Just as you've forgiven yourself, you can forgive others too. You don't have to carry any more resentment. It only hurts you and zaps away your energy. Love yourself, and start seeing where your action or reaction is responsible for whatever position you're in. You cannot change other people, but you can change your response to them. You have a most wonderful gift, freedom of choice. So choose to love and be in harmony rather than in friction or hatred, for your actions will generally be reflected in the other person. Happiness for happiness, anger for anger.

This is a natural law. Natural laws don't play favorites, and, although we can't see them, they work whether we understand them or even believe them. Consider the law of gravity: if you drop a cup, it will fall. It does not care if you knew it would fall or not, or if you dropped it accidentally or purposely. The law is that it will fall.

The law of cause and effect works the same way. It does not care if you're aware or not, it just produces the results from the cause.

With this knowledge, it's prudent to wisely choose constructive behavior if we want good results. An unaware person acting negatively or destructively does not know that they are *creating* negative results, but they produce them anyway. As they become aware of how this law works, they'll want to use it to their advantage by concentrating on constructive change to receive positive results. Irrespective of *their* decisions, you can do what you know in your heart to be right for the benefit of all concerned. Choose carefully the seeds that you want to plant. You can develop your own personality, and become the person you want to be. You don't have to be a carbon copy of someone else. Claim your inheritance and, lovingly, be your own Spirit-given, unique personality.

Choices

Take charge of your mind. It may come as a surprise to you, but you do own your own mind. That's obvious, you say? Then why are we trying to conform to the world of others? Could it be that we have to impress them, otherwise they may not like us the way we are? Are we living the way we want, or the way *they* want us to live? We do have a choice. In fact, the whole of our life is a choice. When we give ourselves permission, we can choose at any given moment what we want to get out of life or put into it. This is what's known as freedom, true freedom.

With true freedom comes the privilege of responsibility, and the strength of growing in our understanding, and the desire to come from a place of calm strength rather than from fear or anger. It includes taking responsibility for our lives and giving up such habits as blaming others.

Blame encourages negativism, resentment, hostility, and escape, so we need to be aware of how we think.

Our brain is like a gyroscope that can keep us on course or off course. It's the incredible computer that has the capability of coming up with all the answers to everything when we tune in to the Universal Power. In fact, it's the process of discovery itself. Scientists have been studying the brain for years, and with every discovery comes the realization of the constant *more* that lies there to be discovered.

We own such a brain. It came to us free. So, perhaps we have no idea of the magnitude of the walking wonder that we are. We're just beginning to scratch the surface of our capabilities. What I am saying is that we are wonderful people, but we have not yet realized it. We're at the beginning of a wonderful discovery—self-discovery. What's kept us from discovering ourselves sooner? The Big Lie. What's the Big Lie? It's the lie that we've bought into believing, and will go to no ends to defend. We will fight for it, kill for it, and get killed for it, yet we don't even want it. The lie is that under our grandiose acts, we believe that we're no good, incapable, a cork bobbing up and down on the ocean of life out of control, an unloved, lonely failure, with others out to get us. The communists, the Arabs, the Irish, the Blacks, the Whites, the neighbor, the mate, the boss— the list is endless.

It's how we see life that makes the difference, and we see it from the way we've been taught to believe it. But we've been taught wrong! Often, we're too proud and lazy, or afraid to go back and discover the truth. We're too scared to admit that we're living a myth. Because we see it, we want to believe in Santa Claus. Just because there's one on every corner doesn't make it real. Our backgrounds have been built on fear. Fear is a lie that appears to be true. That's why we believe it. We live from that viewpoint and it distorts our thinking, actions and results. In Joel Goldsmith's book, *The Art of Meditation,* he states, "Fear is insufficient understanding." Can you agree with that?

Life is a learning process. Painfully, slowly, we learn that what we fear, we bring upon ourselves. So the energy itself is fear, or to put it differently, a wrong way of thinking or seeing things. For example, a child may have had a door closed on her while in a dark closet. It has left her scared of the dark. When, through growing up, therapy, or any other learning experience, she discovers that it was the situation that scared her, she may then no longer be scared of the dark. Nothing has changed, except that she now sees it from a different perspective, and this perspective has freed her from her fear. Think about it. Parents, teachers, religions, nations, employers, commercials, salespeople, knowingly or otherwise, control or manipulate us with fear. When we no longer fear, we remove their control over us.

Perhaps now you say, "Okay, so you've sold me. I can see that fear has held me back, but I'm still afraid. I'd like to change. How can I do that?" We can do that by changing our thinking to believing the truth about ourselves, and looking for the positives instead of the negatives. The truth is that we are like an uncut diamond. The beauty is already there, but it is not recognized until the facets are ground and the light is able to reflect its beauty. We are about to reflect our true beauty by starting to recognize our tremendous potential, by stopping ourselves from selling ourselves short, and by forgiving ourselves for everything and anything that we feel guilty about. Whatever it was belongs to yesterday. Today is a brand new day. Starting from today, it's like we've been given permission to start our lives over afresh, without any prior mistakes. It is important that we do this. So right now, tell yourself, and mean it, that you're sorry that you made whatever those mistakes were. If you will forgive yourself right now, and try not to repeat the mistakes, then you can consider yourself forgiven. Now, take a deep breath, and a sigh of relief that you no longer have to carry that burden of guilt. You've let it go, and you're off to a good start.

Now, let's realize that just as we've made mistakes, others have made mistakes too. Really try to understand that, and try to forgive them also. When we harbor resentments, we hurt ourselves. It keeps us thinking negatively with such things as how to get even with them, to hurt back, or to prove that "I'm right" at any cost. Our pride is rather difficult to control. Know that "the real me" is perfect, and we need to practice being it. There is no need to prove anything. Just know that the more we practice, the better we become at it, and the easier it gets. We will find ourselves trusting ourselves more, and being less influenced by others' opinions. We're beginning to take charge of our lives. This does not mean being closed to other's opinions, but rather making our own decisions to agree or disagree with them. This becomes our responsibility. The results then, are from our actions, so no blame is given to others, freeing us to boost them rather than criticize. As we develop more responsibility for our actions, we will tend to respond to outer influences rather than to react to them. In the past, people were able to control us. We may have resented them and even reacted violently. Now, there's no need to react, but decide how you want to handle the situation.

If I want to upset you and you react to it, I am in control of you. On the other hand, if you say, in effect, "I see what you're doing, but I don't choose to be upset," then you are in charge of you, and I can no longer manipulate you. The key is to realize that you empower yourself, and you do not require the permission of others. You can make the choices of your life. They should be your decisions. The reminder is, "To thine own self be true," first, foremost, and always, with love, courtesy, consideration, and respect for others. I cannot stress too strongly the need to give yourself freedom of choice. It's your heritage, it's your life, and it's the most important part of your evolution, which will result in many rewards. The rewards include confidence in yourself, because you've cut the puppet strings of those trying to control you.

This newly-found freedom enables you to be in charge of your own life, to stop *people-pleasing* for fear that they may not like you. The paradox is that more people will tend to gravitate to you because they envy and appreciate your strength. Everyone loves a winner. People-pleasing says, "I'm a doormat for you to trample on. As long as you will like me or love me, I'll do anything you want me to do." The motivation is fear of losing, fear of loss. The price is usually resentment, both from you and often from the other person. When we come from strength, it says, "I'll love you. I'll be fair with you. But I'll be honest with me, too. Therefore, I hope you continue to love or like me as I grow in my strength and consequent gentleness. I value your love or friendship, and I want it, yet I do not have to have it." This frees resentment and offers a stronger, more honest relationship for understanding and respect.

In desiring my own freedom, I expand this desire for your life, too, offering you every opportunity to grow and expand into being what you want to be, encouraging you to be that in any way that I can. In couples, this may mean for each to grow and expand their individual talents and abilities as well as their togetherness. It's a matter of discovering a healthy balance between being independent as well as being interdependent, which enables both to keep growing.

In former days, the husband kept growing. The wife didn't have, or was not able to take, the opportunity to do so. Consequently, after twenty-five years, the husband became bored with a dull wife and either tolerated her, or left. She, in turn, may have felt lost, alone, and incapable of handling her life, due to selling out to him over the years. This is a sad situation that might have been avoided if each had grown in their independence as well as in their interdependence. To avoid pitfalls, realize that as you develop your independence, those who've dominated you may feel threatened by lack of their control over you. Because you are no longer *people-pleasing,* they may feel insecure, or that they're losing you. It is important at this stage that you communicate your love in words and actions, and honestly share with them their concern, pointing out that your love and caring have not decreased, but that they are taking on a new form, and that in the long run, they can be stronger and more meaningful. It is important that respect, honesty, and communication of your feelings be expressed to each other with a positive approach, with the understanding that this is important for your mutual benefit. It's important, too, to recognize the wonderful person or being that you are, and to draw from that knowledge rather than from fear.

Who Controls Your Thinking and Your Life?

We are like a camera. If we point it at garbage dump and click it, the photo produced is a garbage dump. If we want a picture of a rose, we must aim the camera in that direction, click, and the desired results will be produced. Our actions reflect our thinking, or to put it another way, what we concentrate our thoughts on becomes a reality. It is therefore of prime importance that we filter our thoughts and feelings to be positive and creative, so that our actions create positive results.

The question that we need to ask ourselves is, "Who controls my thoughts?" The obvious answer is, "I do," and that's correct. But knowing this may be only part of the answer. Though it's absolutely true that we control our thoughts, too often we allow others to influence them, and in some cases we become mere puppets in the hands of manipulating people, or bogged down by false concepts or superstitions that we've bought into. Here I have to reiterate the need for great caution, that we not give our minds up to spiritual or religious teachers or gurus, or to our peers or groups, but that we may learn from them, yet be in complete charge of our own thoughts, needs, deeds, and actions. Think for a moment of the influence or superstitions we may be following because of the influence of others. For example, will you walk under a ladder or open an umbrella in the house? Are you prejudiced because that's what you've been taught? If that is the case, have you challenged the concept and grown out of it? What is it that is influencing your thinking, and consequently, running your life for you.

We need to focus our thinking specifically in the direction of what we want to have happen or to experience. To a great extent, we control our destiny. We're in the driver's seat of our lives. Therefore, create your own road map of where you want to go and how you want to live, and follow it using your Spiritual Inner guidance as the light.

Further Understanding

What is it that all of us have, too few express, yet is the one thing that shapes our lives? Songs have been written about it, some share it, others hide it. Think about it for a few moments. You have probably come up with many answers. The answer that I am thinking of is feelings. We have had them suppressed, hurt, buried, smothered, manipulated, and exploited. Doesn't it seem strange that we have had *them* do that to *us?* Whose feelings are they? Who do these feelings belong to, anyway? If my feelings are mine, who is taking responsibility for them? Am I giving permission to others to run my life? Who can possibly know more about me than I do? Where am I with my feelings? Have I dared to look at them? Feared to express them? Questioned why I have them? Felt guilty for having them? Or have I buried them from pain, shame, or from what others may think? Not necessarily logical, is it?

Our feelings are normal and natural. We all have them. They extend from our values, attitudes, and beliefs formulated over the years. These feelings need to be expressed, for if buried, we feel dis-ease, and if buried long enough, they can become a disease. This does not mean that we have a license to hurt or destroy, but that we behave from a controlled action rather than from an uncontrolled reaction. How can we achieve this? Take a deep breath. This helps to slow you down, giving you time to think more clearly and energize yourself with the Creative Force. Practice meditation, so that when you need calm, it will come easier because of your trained discipline. To do this, you might want to sit comfortably, in an upright position, or lie flat on a bed or a couch, or on the floor. Take a slow, deep breath through your nose, first filling your stomach and then your chest with air. Hold it for the count of two, then slowly exhale through your mouth, till there is no more air left in your lungs. Hold it there for a moment. Repeat the process three or four times. Notice how you've calmed. Breathe normally now.

Allow your mind to think of a tranquil scene. Let's imagine the dawning of a beautiful day. Breathe in slowly and smell the air. Relax into the arms of nature as it cradles you in its womb of peace. All is well, and we know that *Peace towards all mankind begins with me, and that right now I am at peace with the world, myself and my Creator. I can come back to this meditative place any time I choose. I now feel relaxed and harmonious. I take another deep breath and let it out. I get up slowly and take a nice, comfortable stretch. I feel strengthened, invigorated and alert, ready to make the most of my Spiritual Power's generous gift to me—this day!*

CHAPTER NINE

Constructive Action

Being Assertive

How we see people makes a difference. In your mind, separate the person from their action. Try to remember that if they were more aware, they would be behaving differently. Let this be a discernment on your part and not a judgment. Be aware that your practice of understanding will not only serve you well, but will also offer others a mirror of their actions, showing them an alternative choice that they could use in the future.

As an example, an office manager may be feeling upset because she is being criticized by her employer. You happen to be the next person she comes across, and she cowardly vents her frustration on you. Should you react to her behavior, you'd compound the problem. However, by taking a deep, calm breath, and being in control, you might say, "I don't know why you're angry at me. I'm feeling frustrated because I'm giving you of my best. If there is a specific problem I may have overlooked, I'll be happy to cooperate and remedy it, as my intention is to do my job as efficiently as I can and to support you with my expertise."

What you have done is shown her your ability to communicate your feelings by being true to yourself, and relieved some of her hostility or fear by showing that you are understanding of her behavior and that you desire to be cooperative. Again, the rule of thumb is, "To thine own self be true, first, foremost, and always, with love, understanding, consideration, and respect for others." This may not always be easy, but it is wise and necessary, so that we can learn the art of assertiveness and how to create balance in our lives. Let's enjoy our freedom, express our uniqueness, and grow. For me, this is the whole purpose of life: learning how to grow to overcome hostilities, pettiness, and bickering, and to view problems as opportunities not yet recognized. Remember, we may not be responsible for what we feel, but only we can be responsible for what we do with our feelings.

It has been said that love conquers all. If we could but love ourselves enough, and recognize and accept the beauty in ourselves, it would overflow and show, enabling us to truly love our neighbors as ourself, and end strife, wars, and conflict, thereby creating a utopia. Are we loving our Spiritual-selves enough to do this? *Love begins with me*, each one of us, and like a pebble thrown into a pond, it ripples ever outward, ever expanding, favorably affecting others. By living from or responding with love, I use wisdom and understanding, changing that which I can and accepting that which I cannot change. By responding with love, it's returned, and I receive more love. The natural law is impartial. It returns to us what we put out. It does not play favorites. That's why pretending to be loving when we're burning up inside does not work. It has to be honest.

Everything's a matter of how we perceive it. If we think *the world's out to get me*, then for us it's very real, frightening, and true, for it's what we believe. Therefore, what we believe is true for us, but it's not necessarily truth. With wisdom comes truth, and we begin to see and understand. For example, if we change our thinking away from *the world's out to get me*, it no longer is. The point is, we cannot change the things "out there." We need to see that the different responses, viewpoints, and choices that we make affect our lives. Stop blaming the circumstance or the other person, become responsible for your own actions, and realize that it is your actions that can change your circumstances. You have to be able to see that from deep down inside of you, so that this realization becomes natural. If you do not like the tape you are playing, you can replace it with the tape of life that you want to play from now on, but you have to do it and not merely dream about doing it. So, do it now.

"Love Project" Principles

One factor that seems to confuse us is that life is full of paradoxes. To have electricity, there has to be a negative pole and a positive pole. Paradoxes tend to make things inclusive rather than exclusive. When we grasp this and expand our outlook from a *this-or-that* attitude to a *this-and-that* attitude, it becomes inclusive rather than exclusive. Destiny has the same characteristic. It is not either/or.

There is a destiny, and we create our own destiny. It offers us unlimited choices that we may not have been aware of having. I discovered this dramatically, and my personal growth took off and expanded rapidly, due in large part to The Love Project, now called The Telos Institute. You can write to them c/o The Teleos Institute, P.O. Box 12009-418, Scottsdale, Arizona, 85267; 602-391-0726. They have many books, tapes, and classes which I recommend, and they'll send you a flyer of them upon request if you wish to have one. They also have six Love Project principles that I'd like to share with you, and then comment on each of the principles

- Be the change you want to see happen, instead of trying to change everyone else.
- Receive all persons as beautiful (including self) exactly where they are.
- Provide others with the opportunity to give.
- Perceive problems as opportunities.
- Have no expectations, but rather abundant expectancy.
- Create your own reality consciously, rather than living as if you had no control over your life.

Create your own reality consciously, rather than living as if you had no control over your life, i.e., being a victim. Until we learn otherwise, it might seem natural to be a victim. After all, what can one do?

I was brought up to be humble. To me, being humble was being a people pleaser. From a victim belief, everyone was more important than I. Therefore, they counted but I didn't—you know, the doormat syndrome. This caused a lot of inside frustration building up and festering until, much to my horror, I would finally, when some minor last straw fell, explode into a built-up rage. This would be followed by, of course, enormous guilt and overcompensatory niceness in order to be a very good person again. What a vicious circle. Why did this happen? I guess it was because I didn't know that I could create my own reality. I was like a cork bobbing up and down on the ocean, hopeless and helpless. I believed what helped me overcome this situation was discovering another Love Project Principle.

Be the change that you want to see happen, instead of trying to change everyone else. I learned that I didn't have to remain a victim. When you walk around with a sign on you that says "Kick me!" people oblige. When you remove the sign, it stops. You control the sign that you put up. Until I learned this, I had no self-esteem. What also helped me was to learn that I was created to be equal with others, no greater, but no less, either. I had to discover and learn to love myself as well as others. If I didn't have love in me or for me, how could I possibly give it to others? If I didn't give it, how could I possibly expect to get it returned to me?

I then discovered a wonderful thing called *freedom of choice.* You can do anything you want. But remember that real freedom carries the price tag of responsibility, and everything has consequences. What you sow, you reap. It's wise to sow love. What also becomes very apparent is that everything isn't just black and white, but different shades of grey. There are more than just the options of *this-or-that.* There are thousands of options, as many as your imagination can come up with. As the captain of my ship, I can choose any of them, and if that choice doesn't seem to be right, I can instantly make other choices. What an exciting way to live, to be responsible for my own actions. This gave me such energy. Whereas before I would blame others and try in vain to change them, I now use that energy and time constructively. Blame never solves problems, it just creates them. Have you ever succeeded in changing someone else? It's a lesson in futility.

Two extremely important elements in making choices are our attitudes and our motives. If I elect to have a negative attitude, my choices and subsequent results will be negative, because I've sown the seeds of negativity. The law is like the soil. It doesn't care what you plant; it will give you what you plant. The law just says yes to everything:

"I am no good."

"Yes, if that's what you choose to believe," the law answers.

"I am confident and capable."

"Yes, of course you are," it says.

The biblical quote is, "It is done to you as you believe in your heart." Is my motive to deceive for personal gain at any price because of greed, lust, and selfishness? Or is it for purity of purpose, the best and highest good for myself and for all others included? Principles are sometimes hard to live up to, but the consequences of not doing so are ultimately so much worse. The purest motive is not fear, but a heart of love. This leads to the next Love Project principle.

Receive all persons as beautiful exactly where they are. I struggled for about ten years with this principle. How could I possibly receive a terrible person the same as a beautiful person exactly the way they are? I had to judge them, it seemed. It seemed impossible to accept that principle, although it haunted me constantly. Finally I got the message. Aha, now I see. What brought the dawning? (I'm struggling with my conscience as to whether to give you my answer or let you struggle to learn it for yourself, because my experiences are my experiences and yours may be different.) I came to realize that we are all part of nature and that there's an energy common to each of us. We are tied together by a common denominator, the Universal Power. We are literally bonded within as brothers and sisters. Our differences are that we have been created to be unique so as to give our unique genius to the world and the world family as a gift of our gratitude for life. Because of our genes, upbringing, understanding, or lack of understanding, brought about by our life's experiences or programming, our beliefs vary.

The terrorist, from his viewpoint, is a hero. He can't see what we see, that he's misguided. He's temporarily blinded. Had we been able to see some of the mistakes that we've made, perhaps we wouldn't have made them either. We need to separate the heart of the person from their actions. I cannot condone the action, but I can love the heart that I know to be pure, even if the other person hasn't yet recognized it. We're all on a journey of self-discovery. Some are more advanced than others, some of us lag behind. By loving the heart energy in others, it may help them discover it in themselves. By condemning them, it creates a fight or flight position, in order for them to prove that they are right. When we become truly aware of what love is, we discover that we can be our unique selves, and by being true to ourselves, we have nothing to prove. In other words, you can condemn me for being guilty, but if I know that I'm not guilty, your opinion is just that, your opinion. It has nothing to do with me, so I don't give energy to the lie by fighting it.

Perceive problems as opportunities. Without problems we probably would not learn very much. Problems can pull us down completely if we let them, but if we view them as opportunities for growth, we can strengthen ourselves to work through them satisfactorily rather than seeking drugs, alcohol, and other escapes that complicate the situation and create more problems. Problems come in two forms, those that we seemingly have no control over, such as climate, earthquakes, and other natural occurrences, and those that we create for ourselves—and with our normal thinking, actions, and reactions, we create plenty.

There's much talk today about how bad some tension is for our health. If we examine our tensions closely we will find that we can control many of them. For example, Mary had a job about thirty minutes from her home, and she usually left her house at the last minute, lane hopping to get there on time. Arriving tense, there was no time for her to relax. She carried the tension with her, compounding it throughout the day. Were she to leave ten minutes earlier, she could take it easy, arrive on time, have a few minutes to herself, and start to relax. It takes examination and self-discipline to look at the benefits versus the alternatives, and either choice is okay, for it's your life to live the way you choose. I like the serenity prayer. It's so powerful: *God grant me the serenity to accept the things I cannot change, the courage to change the things that I can, and the wisdom to know the difference.*

One of the unconscious things that we tend to do is to set ourselves up for disappointments. This can be easily prevented by applying the next Love Project principle.

Have no expectations but rather abundant expectancy. Maybe we've experienced looking forward so much to seeing a movie that won a lot of academy awards, only to be let down because we didn't find it exceptional. We do this with our relationships, too. We so much want the other person to be a perfect dream that we place them high on a pedestal so that it's impossible for them to live up to those expectations. Then, when they let us down, we are disappointed, and often critical or bitter. Having abundant expectancy is having preferences rather than demands. You can still strive for what you want, yet not be shattered if you don't get it.

Provide others with the opportunity to give. You need to ask for what you want, as people are not mind readers. If you want something, it's your responsibility to ask for it. They can't provide it if they don't know that you want it. For example, I want permission from the Love Project to include their principles in this book. I'm providing them with the opportunity to give me that permission. I have no expectations but abundant expectancy. I have since obtained permission from them, for which I am truly grateful.

Transmuting Fear

Peace is a state of harmony. Wherever there are imbalances, enlightenment is available. I feel this to be a breakthrough. Although we have talked about peace for centuries, I question why we have not yet attained it? Perhaps our feelings are the clues to an important discovery? Usually women have allowed themselves the freedom to express their feelings, which often got them into trouble by loving, enabling, being emotional, crying, being out-of-control, and that earned them the reputation of being the weaker sex. Usually men have had to shut down their feelings. "Big boys don't cry like women, or change their minds. You need to be a protector, macho, a rock of Gibraltar, the leader of the family, one who always knows what's right and best." Both of these approaches, of course, are ancient now, but our fear and our feelings, our emotions, have kept us from peace.

If we dig deeply enough, we will discover that fear causes all of our problems, but for now, let's concentrate on our feelings. From the above two examples, we're between a rock and a hard place. If we give in to our feelings we're in trouble, and if we bury our feelings we're in trouble. Is there a solution? Very definitely, yes. If we can understand and attain it, perhaps we'll have found the missing ingredient, the absence of which has prevented us from attaining peace.

Let's be open to examining alternative concepts. The old ones haven't worked, so we need to explore, grow, and solve the problems. First, we need to accept that our feelings are okay. They are nothing to feel ashamed about. They may not even be rational, and they may come to us whether we want them to or not. For example, I may have sexual feelings toward a relative's wife. I'm too ashamed to admit this even to myself, much less share it with someone else. So what do I do with it? I bury it. I pretend and lie to myself that it didn't even happen, because I want to be good, and how can I be good if I have such terrible feelings. Or, I feel that I want to do somebody bodily harm, but of course, I can't let that happen, so I bury it. Pretty soon I have a graveyard full of fear that I can't tell anyone about. So I suffer the secrets of guilt and shut down. Dishonestly I put on a front that all is okay, but I feel uptight inside. My body knows the truth and is trying to tell me to let it out, but I'm too scared to listen.

We need to face our fears, and that takes work. We try to escape this work by various escape mechanisms, such as drugs, alcohol, sex, gambling, something, anything to distract ourselves from looking into our closet of fear and dealing with it once and for all. Maybe we don't like our thoughts or our feelings the way they are, so what can we do with them? First, we have to stop being in denial and realize that feelings or thoughts are energy. Energy is something that's happening or waiting to happen, to manifest. This energy can be transmuted and changed, but it has to go somewhere. It needs to be redirected. Rather than let our emotions run wild, or shut them down, we need to:

1) Recognize and admit that they exist. The feelings are there whether we like them or not.

2) Be honest and admit to them.

3) Know that they need to be dealt with.

Options: Discuss your feeling with someone who is capable, someone you can trust.

Ask for Inner guidance.

Don't feel guilty or judgmental about your feelings. Feelings are just feelings that need to be examined.

If your feelings are hostile, expend that energy on taking a walk or playing tennis, or on some other constructive interest. What you've chosen to do is use that energy to your advantage to accomplish something that you might not otherwise have done. So the energy, because of your redirection of it, has been helpful. And your emotion, instead of being carried out in its original form or being buried, has been transmuted into a positive action, defusing its fear and hold on you, and becoming an asset in your life. Now, feeling clean for having dealt with it, you genuinely feel good, and having learned how to deal with it, you no longer fear your feelings. Because of your constructive redirection of them, you can now welcome your feelings to help you accomplish things in your life, which without this extra energy you might not have experienced. You now feel good about yourself, and no longer threatened.

When you're not feeling threatened (fear), you come from a faith or strength that does not need to prove itself, and you can therefore be strong, gentle, effective, and open to other experiences. Without these fears, we can open to allow other people into our lives. When we're open to let others in, with all the joys and sorrows that it may entail, we begin living life fully, accepting ourselves and learning to love ourselves and others unconditionally, discerning their actions and reactions, but not judging the person.

Coming from a place of non-judgment enables us to encourage others in constructive directions without their feeling threatened. When they're not feeling threatened, they no longer have to react to judgment to try to prove themselves right or to get angry, and instead can use the energy to improve themselves, encouraged by your being for them rather than against them. This helps release a positive and constructive energy which, in turn, changes fear and aggressiveness to understanding. Understanding and maturity bring with them inclusiveness rather than exclusiveness. Inclusiveness creates peace and love, which is what life and joy is all about. One helpful way to accomplish harmony is to study conflict resolution so we can openly express what we feel and what we need. When we're clear, we send a clear message enabling others to respond to what we want, rather than making them guess what is going on in our head.

Anger

I was told, "I love you; you understand me." Understanding the other person is a mirror of self-understanding. If I'm aware of what makes me tick, or what's going on inside of me, it becomes less difficult to understand others. Basically, people have similar needs and feelings. Underneath the masks, the upbringing and experiences that life has brought them, they want love, security, happiness, companionship, and acceptance as a person. When we act unkindly towards another person, it is because we recognize our differences rather than our similarities. We need to unlearn this habit and look for what encompasses rather than that which divides us. With this understanding we can realize that when someone is acting up, it's usually because they don't know how to cope with a situation and their confusion makes them angry.

Instead of responding to the outward scene, if we are aware, we will realize that they are calling out for our love and understanding to get them out of this mess. The paradox is that no one else can really help. It's for each person to discover for him/herself.

Let's start by realizing how the body functions. Unconsciously, we breathe, move, and think, almost automatically. The marvels that make this possible have been built in, and we take them for granted. Also built in is the ability to cope, but this is not recognized until one becomes aware. What is awareness, and how is it discovered? Then, is it worth the effort to learn? Well, look at the alternatives. If we're not satisfied, isn't it worth trying another approach?

When many of us are unhappy, we blame others for our troubles, fully convinced that because they did this or said that to us, we are now suffering. For example, Bill told his wife Mary that he wanted to have his manager and his wife over for dinner on Tuesday night. Mary, realizing that Bob was due for a promotion, agreed (wrong motive), but after the evening was over, she was exhausted and upset with Bob for not arranging it for a Saturday night when she could have had the day to prepare, plus probably have had his help. This frustration became anger that she expressed by blaming him for being inconsiderate of her. What was required here was honesty and communication. Mary could have expressed her feelings much earlier by saying, "Bob, I get so upset with you when you don't seem to consider me and make midweek dinner arrangements. I want to love you and not be upset with you. So won't you please consider my needs also?" Mary might have added that she'd love to have Tom and his wife over for dinner on Saturday evening when she'd have time to prepare, and not have to panic after work on Tuesday by trying to get dinner ready while fighting the clock. With such pressure, it would be difficult to enjoy the evening.

With this awareness, Bob may have elected to postpone dinner until Saturday evening. This way, Mary, sharing her feelings honestly, would have been looking after her needs and seeking cooperation, rather than burying what could become a volcano ready to erupt, bringing her just the opposite results of what she wanted. We can be in charge of our lives, harmoniously, when we know how and take the courage to do it. What we were not aware of is that we did not need to be a victim and let the other person do this to us. We can be, and need to be, in charge of ourselves and our communication. *I am the only one who can be directly responsible for me, and only for me. I cannot be responsible for the other's actions, even though I may have tried.* Each person is responsible for himself/ herself. I do not mean this to create separation, but just the contrary. As people realize this, we'll become more understanding of how to live and let live.

Anger Gets You Mad

Anger can create constructive action, but more often it creates destructive energy in the form of a temper, and temper perpetuates itself.

There are many therapies advocating the use of anger. In some special cases it may be necessary to express deep-seated anger before one can communicate, but for most of us to concentrate on ridding our anger is a mistake. Before you get angry with me for this statement, read on, hopefully with an open mind. Please note I did not say deny your anger, nor did I say bottle up your anger, for it would be unhealthy to do either. To constantly try to control your anger only ends up in an explosion of temper. I know. I fought a losing battle for years, trying to control my temper.

Let's examine why anger doesn't work. How do we learn to do anything? We practice. If it's piano, we learn the notes and practice over and over hitting the keys. Usually, the more practice, the more perfectly we play. We learn through repetition. If we are constantly angry, by being angry we become more proficient at expressing it, usually in the form of a temper. It certainly doesn't make for happy living, and we get deeper and deeper into it, like a dog chasing its own tail. We get angry, then we feel guilty. We overcompensate for the guilt and get angry again. More of the same is a lesson in futility.

When we're angry, there's a lot of meaning to the saying, "I'm so mad." Mad, temporarily insane, out of control. Now look at why you're upset. Are others making you angry? If you feel this is the reason, you will react in anger. Are you angry because you feel inferior, not up to the job? Is it anger or fear that is getting to you? Remember, everything stems from fear, if we trace it back far enough. Have you depended on somebody and they've let you down? Are you after revenge to get even with them? Frustrating, isn't it? Track back a little. In the long run, has your being angry helped you? Be honest with yourself. It might have stimulated your energy and made you feel more alive, but has it been beneficial? It hasn't worked, has it? Neither has blaming others. Admit it, and climb out of the quicksand. Don't get swallowed up by it, struggling more and more with the determination to stop it. The more determined you are to stop, the more you think about it. The more you struggle with it, the deeper it gets ingrained into your subconscious mind, and the more you keep repeating the error.

I don't know that we'll ever overcome anger completely. In my own experience, I didn't understand myself and consequently didn't know how to deal with people. I couldn't handle conflict. I wanted to be a nice person. As I have mentioned already, I became a people pleaser. Do you have any idea what that did to me on the inside? I'd give in to keep the peace, resenting the consequences and burying my anger.

However, we are responsible for our own actions, so instead of merely reacting to a situation with anger, we need to learn to respond with a calm strength. It is not something you can force yourself to do. It comes with practice, as we learn to see things with understanding. Understanding is an awareness of yourself and of others. It will bring you strength as you assume responsibility for your own thoughts and actions, so that you no longer need to blame others or react to outside manipulation. To overcome anger, we need to face it squarely and honestly and take complete responsibility for it, whether it seems our fault or not. Quite a statement, isn't it? You ask, "Why should *I* be responsible, when it's them doing it to me?" And the reason, of course, is that *I can do something about myself, but I cannot control others.*

What can one do? First, recognize your feelings and admit the fact that you are feeling angry. Next, try to find a positive outlet for angry feelings. It may mean taking walks, running, working out in a gym, playing music, something constructive to calm you down. At such times do not drink coffee or alcohol or take drugs. Do not drive or do any dangerous activities that require full and calm concentration, which you're currently not capable of in your angered state. To get calm, take a few deep breaths to quiet your mind and body. Then check: is the anger serving your purpose or defeating it? Try to see the upsetting problem from the viewpoint of an observer who is not emotionally involved. What constructive options do you see?

Remember, *you have choices.* You don't have to remain stuck. Only you can decide that you've expended enough negative energy and then make the necessary changes.

Discovery

Inherent in all of us are the ultimate questions, "Who am I?" "Why am I here?" "What is life all about?" "What's life's purpose?" It's for us to understand that the Universal Power is the purpose of life and that we're just temporarily visiting this planet as a stepping stone to understanding the Higher Consciousness that we already are. Instead of gain, competition, and *me at all costs,* we must come to realize that understanding is essential. If this realization comes to the whole family at once, then they are very blessed. But if it just hits one member, their test of fate may be a very hard one, for their spiritual experience will teach them a life very different from the earthly existence that they have been used to. This change is gratefully welcomed, but until the understanding reaches the rest of the family, it may pose a real threat.

To begin with, if we think of life without our Spiritual Power, there's real insecurity. Add to that insecurity the thought of making a change to an intangible way of living and a belief in the unseen, and fear of change becomes even greater, which often expresses itself in resentment and rejection of the newly-aware person, in the forms of hostility, ridicule, anger, and frustration: "You're crazy!" "The whole world's wrong except you?" And the attacks may go on.

"Go out and compete like others, lazy." "You don't love me because you don't dote on me, having replaced me with a real God."

It may be hard for you to cope with receiving all this abuse, yet once you start on the spiritual journey, there's no turning back. It is a time for courage and strength, rather than to react to your partner's insecurity.

Now is an opportunity to stand firm, yet it's essential to demonstrate more love and understanding by sharing with your partner that as you grow in your understanding, the changes can be of more benefit for both of you, and that whereas you will be considerate of your partner, you have to be true and honest to yourself also and follow your drummer, which can bring more love and understanding. In the long run, love and honesty is healthier than trying to please others.

CHAPTER TEN

Attitudes

Attitudes and Healing

WE ALL HAVE ATTITUDES. Some of them are good, some not so good. If there is one thing more than circumstances that governs your life, it is attitude. With the right attitude, you can create the right circumstances. With the wrong attitude, circumstances control you, with continual ups and downs. Be in charge of your attitude; let it work for you to attract the positive.

The importance of our attitude is that it affects our happiness and our health, as well as our relationships with others. Most people react to life, mirroring back others' attitudes. If life isn't treating us right, perhaps instead of blaming everyone else, we need to take a look at ourselves.

Because of our different experiences in life, we see people differently. One person loves Tommy, and the other person thinks Tommy is terrible. We just project our own views, judgments, and labeling of him, good or bad. Tommy is Tommy, but how we see him differs. The more we understand ourselves, the easier it is to understand others and to separate out our projections from the real Tommy. We can then become less judgmental, which results in a healthier attitude. When, instead of blaming others, I take responsibility for my own actions, I use my freedom of choice. I become captain of my own destiny, choosing to respond from my highest understanding, rather than reacting.

An understanding that the Universal Power *IS* within each of us tells us to look within ourselves for the truth, and to respect the truth in others, no matter how deeply it appears to be buried. Therefore we can let the Spiritual Power's love, within ourselves and others, reflect goodwill towards all humankind, irrespective of race, color, creed, or religion, and not merely just over a holiday season, but every day.

If you are guilty about something, look at it and understand it, and decide to behave differently in the future. Above all, forgive yourself right now. Go forward into a brand new day. The darkness belongs to yesterday, and yesterday is over. Embrace and live in today. It's here for you *NOW*. Tomorrow hasn't yet arrived.

This next part may seem difficult. We need to forgive everybody for all the terrible things, the hurts and the frustrations, that they have caused us. Really, we ought to be grateful to them, because they have made things so bad that we have desperately looked or been forced to look for alternatives. If they hadn't done those things, we might still be reacting to life, controlled by the elements. But now we have discovered the gifts of choice and are taking charge of our own lives. The newly-found freedom is not rampant or irresponsible.

Because we are no longer willing to let others manipulate us, we are aware and cautious not to manipulate others. As we become in charge of where we are going in our lives, it becomes less necessary for us to live in the old habit patterns. We no longer have to prove ourselves to get the approval of others. We're now in charge of ourselves. Give yourself permission to bring out the best in yourself, whether others appreciate it or not, for deep down the real you is good and beautiful. Keep peeling the onion skin. Remove the layers of hurts, frustrations, hates, prejudices, and resentments. Keep seeking *you*, the pearl of great price.

Self-Help

Some years ago I was counseling a lady in her mid-twenties. She was recently divorced and indicated to me that something had been missing. There had been no love in her marriage. As we continued, she told me that her parents had not shown love and that she didn't know how to love, a fact that she had not wanted to admit even to herself. Denial is an illusion that needs to be overcome if we are to cure ourselves of our problems. In drug and alcohol prevention classes, the heavy smoker or alcoholic is often in denial and will claim that they can quit tomorrow. There is no longer a stigma attached to the sickness of being addicted. The fact is that an alcoholic needs treatment, just as a broken leg would need treatment. We have to get honest with ourselves.

Honesty is the bottom line for all good treatment. Recognize the problem, do not dwell on it, and start climbing out of the pit. Sometimes this requires competent help. While searching for the cause of our problems, we sometimes unfortunately dig a pit and keep digging and wallowing in it. Others of us dig one foot, loosen the soil, plant new seeds of change, and nurture them. Frequently, as people face themselves, they indicate the lack of love and touching shown to them, so they in turn find great difficulty in expressing their own feelings. Again, recognition and admission is a big factor, followed by the desire to change our attitudes, thinking, and consequent behavior. Because you may not have experienced love in your life thus far, does not mean that you cannot love.

The big question might be, "How does one love?" Perhaps it starts by beginning to appreciate yourself. Try this experiment. Please do it, and do it now. Take two sheets of paper. On the first write down all the positive statements that you can think of about yourself. "I am . . . ta da ta da ta da." Okay. Now on the second sheet of paper write down all the negative statements about yourself. Many people find that sheet number one has very few statements, but that sheet number two wasn't even big enough to fill in all your negative statements. Take a good look at sheet two. Now tear it up and throw it in the recycling trash where it belongs, and forget it.

Take page one again and start concentrating on filling it up. This is the thinking to be concentrating on. There is a lot of truth in "as we think, so we become." As we learn to accept our good and look for that, we begin to do the same in looking at others. We then become more interested, and more interesting, to them. As we feel better about ourselves, we gain confidence enough to give ourselves permission to see the beauty in ourselves. This is not egotistical. We really are perfect, beautiful, and whole, a child of the Universal Nature, created in the spirit of God, and we are of that same Essence. Our sin or error has been in not believing this. How can anything made of perfection be less than perfect? It is our lack of understanding that has had us living from fear. Therefore, the more accepting I can be of me, the less I need to rely on other's approval of me for me to feel good, and the more honest I can be with myself by not bottling up my frustrations. I can then begin to share my thinking and feelings openly, and, because I share myself, I can listen and hear others, and encourage their good, too. This creates ever more blessings.

What I Think Is Important

One of the best things we can do for our health is to be happy and bring joy into our lives and into the lives of others. I enjoy living optimistically and talking that way, because I know this works best in my life. That does not mean, however, that we who are optimistic are without our share of problems or that we hide from them. Quite the contrary is true. We face them, deal with them the best we can, and continue living. What does *as best I can* mean? To me, it starts with my belief system. If I view problems as opportunities in disguise, then I can appreciate these opportunities as hurdles to be cleared for my growth. If you doubt this, look back at some problem that you've satisfactorily overcome and answer honestly. Although, perhaps you wouldn't like to reexperience it again, haven't you grown and learned from this experience? I'm sure that your answer is yes. However, if I'm convinced that *they're out to get me,* that's the way it's going to appear. It's as if we are holding a magnet to attract problems, and it does. What I'm saying is, our actions follow our thoughts, which have a great deal to do with what goes on *out there.* It's as if our mind constantly says yes to us. It does not care what the question is, it just says "yes." For example,

"I feel low."

"Yes, you are."

"This is a beautiful day."

"Yes, it is."

"Life is marvelous."

"Yes."

"Life is full of troubles."

"Yes."

Our thoughts, words, and feelings are the part of our destiny that we create. We need to be aware and claim our responsibility for this, and filter what we take in or believe, think, and act upon. Our self-talk, what we're telling ourselves, is what we're creating. Our words are very powerful and get mirrored back to us. Criticize others, and they will oblige in the same manner. Genuinely care about others, and they will respond quickly in a like manner. It's not magic. It just seems that way. What we dwell on in our thoughts becomes real. It behooves us to get our thinking right. Replace negative thinking with positive thoughts.

Become optimistic, and see your world changing for the better. Enjoy your blessings. Seek them out. Look at your body with its incredible mechanisms, and appreciate the miracle of your life. Then start looking for other blessings. Appreciate yourself. Show and tell your appreciation of others, and don't wait until they're buried to do so. And if they already are, don't spend your time feeling guilty about it now. It belongs to the past. Yesterday is finished. Today is a new day. Be in charge of your life. Express your views and your uniqueness. Empower yourself; it's important. You count. Give thanks to your Spiritual Power, and let this light shine through you to express your deepest beauty. Start now, and see the difference.

In Norman Cousins' book, *Anatomy of an Illness,* he explains how he was incurably ill and laughed himself back to health. He then taught the doctors at UCLA. You can bring joy and happiness into your life. Don't wait for someone else to do it. They can't. It has to come from you.

Broadening Horizons

Broadening our horizons can be a challenge leading to a life of happiness. Do you remember the old cart horses, plodding down the street, bearing blinders which restricted vision only to the front? How many of us live our lives in such a restricted manner? One of the attitudes of being loving is to be giving, and it's important to see just what it is that we are giving. We lose our happiness when we cater to everyone else, forgetting to love and be true to ourselves. We also lose happiness when we go out to destroy our neighbors by pulling them apart with criticism, or trying to make them over by manipulating them to conform to our demands, especially if those demands happen to be bigoted, unreasonable, or unfair. Nobody wins in these situations, and often the victims are hurt or even crushed.

I am suggesting, *victims awaken*. If you'll stop allowing yourselves to be victims, there won't be anyone to bully. Let those who choose to be miserable be miserable, but don't you be affected by this. If enough of you don't react, the would-be oppressors may learn from their mistakes and choose to start living differently, enjoying life for themselves and bringing joy, not misery to others. If we would only realize that life is a mirror that reflects back to us what we put out, common sense would tell us to do unto others as we'd like them to do to us. Although a purer motive would be more desirable, the results and benefits you'll derive will astound you. Critical persons can change and grow to love and accept themselves. It is easy when we stop judging, feeling guilty and unworthy, and recognize that deep down in our depths, we are perfection. Love this perfection and it will emerge. The song suggests, "Accentuate the positive, eliminate the negative." So no matter how you may have behaved by using criticism, meanness, and dishonesty, that all belongs to yesterday. Forgive yourself right now, and start each brand new day by becoming the change you want to see happen. In just a few weeks, you'll find yourself glowing and wondering how you ever could have lived differently. Part of our life's experience is to learn from our mistakes and to correct them. It's all a matter of growing through it, and knowing and accepting our oneness with our Spiritual Nature will make it easier.

Gratitude and Appreciation

Spring has sprung. How magnificent it is to see the profusion of flowers, with their special scents and spectacular colors, popping up out of the ground to wish us a cheery "Hello," whenever we take the time to look at them. What a delightful time of year this is, as nature once again reminds us that all is new, and to awaken to this beautiful day, to whistle and sing like the birds. The winter of yesterday lies dormant as the miracle of today beckons us to recognize it as the dawning opportunity of Now.

For the young, there's the opportunity to grow, explore, make mistakes, correct them, and learn that life is to be lived, enjoyed, appreciated, and shared, and that there's more to life than *me* alone. There are others to be considered, too! It's not too early for them, like some of their elders, to ponder on the mysteries of life, its blessings and its purpose. To do this, we need to have an open mind as life-styles, ideas, and thoughts change. Like spring, there is always the exciting new. Sometimes that difference feels scary, but look deeper. Just perhaps we might be looking at the new with old ideas.

For example, we used to think that to love ourselves meant to be vain, conceited, egotistical, or a braggadocio. Today, to love our-selves means to understand ourselves, to know that the Spiritual Nature is within us, and that therefore we are worthy. A great book says, "Love thy neighbor as thyself," implying to love yourself, your highest and best self. When I can accept and love myself, only then can I truly love my neighbor. I cannot give love if I don't have it, so it behooves me to train myself to be loving and kind.

One of our goals in growing is to recognize our value. We are not second-rate citizens. In a non-egotistical way, we are very important, and as we gain this understanding, we learn to become assertive. And herein lies a potential trap. We may become so assertive that we go right past being assertive and become aggressive. When becoming independent or assertive, it is essential to bring with it more love, not less love. Real strength doesn't have to prove anything.

Think of your positive and pleasant friends, people you know. What traits or habits do they have that appeal to you? Chances are that those assets would work for you, too. I have created a list of positive and constructive traits to seek (please see Appendix A). The list includes many of the traits that bring joy and happiness into our lives. I'm sure that you have encountered many of the ones that I have listed.

I have also created a list to share with you of some of the traits that are the problem ones (refer to Appendix B). What you might do is look at them and see if any of them are part of your personality, then try and rid yourself of them. Trade them for the positive ones. Let go of the things that don't work. Some of them are real joykillers.

So, comparing the two lists, the things that cause happiness versus the things that bring unhappiness, might help you to view the way you want to live. The choice is always yours!

Responsibility

Constantly, outside circumstances unexpectedly occur to affect our lives. Someone calls with a suggestion to go to a movie. A friend drops in from out of town. I planned to sunbathe, but it started raining. I was going to be there in fifteen minutes, but the car had a flat tire or wouldn't start. I could go on and on with outside influences that affect me. Therefore, if I plan my life, I can be sure that unexpected things may interfere to change my plans.

There are unlimited choices that I can make in coping with each unexpected influence. How I cope with these circumstances depends upon a combination of my attitude, my experience, my beliefs, my own imprisonment or freedom, my understanding, my choices, and my choice of ego or wisdom. Among the multiple choices that I have, I can react to a circumstance emotionally, with an attitude of blame such as "You made me late!", or I can welcome the intrusions by being aware that the unexpected is really to be expected and accept it as part of my growing experience, which is what life is all about. The intrusion, then, becomes an opportunity to be dealt with and learned from. How I deal with it affects my life, and indirectly, the lives of others.

By reacting with fear, force, hatred, or resentment, I encourage these actions or feelings to grow faster, and they boomerang to hurt me. By responding with love, I use wisdom and understanding, changing that which I can and accepting that which I cannot change. By responding with love, it, too, boomerangs, and I receive more love. The natural law is impartial. It returns to us what we put out. It does not play favorites. That's why pretending to be loving while we're burning up inside does not work. We have to be honest.

CHAPTER ELEVEN

Love

On Love

IN A CRAZED WORLD OF VIOLENCE, where we excel in creating killing machines, where hunger and homelessness prevail, and where drugs, alcohol, and dysfunctional families are prevalent, there has to be a solution. And that solution is Peace. You may well ask, "How is peace obtainable?" It requires a massive, mature education of principles that work, the foundation of which is love, caring, concern, and constructive action.

Our emphasis on mature education needs to start with relationships, using respect and responsibility in individual behavior, and using conflict resolution to respond to one another, rather than reacting with hostility and force. We need to develop a high self-esteem, with reverence for the Universal Power from whence it all stems. We need to let go of competition and start blending and harmonizing for the benefit of all, becoming inclusive rather than exclusive.

Love would solve all our problems. "But it will never happen," you say. Exactly. It will never happen as long as you believe it will never happen. That is the reason we need this education, to strengthen our courage to change that belief to one of realizing that it can happen. Indeed, it must happen. Everyone's clamoring for love. It's a built in requirement. If we lack love, we feel neglected, alone, uncared for, inadequate, and unable to cope. This is why we buy everything in sight to try and fill our emptiness, to bring us happiness. But things don't substitute for love, and soon we're out buying more, always more. But it never satisfies.

How can we love if all we've learned is distrust, disgust, dysfunction, helplessness, and despair—or greed, lying, and cheating? How can we love if, because of poverty, our minds have been on food, shelter, and survival; or if we believe that to survive we must be tough, violent, and cheat in business for power, greed, and money (as demonstrated by the savings and loan bailouts and others who continue to be allowed to bilk us while they receive only a light reprimand)?

Love is simple, but it is not easy to attain until we can see its benefits and want it. We are then prepared to change to constructive thinking, using our freedom of choice to obtain what we want, rather than remaining a victim of circumstances. It takes courage to make changes, but since what we have is not satisfactory, we have to use our courage for constructive changes. We each have within us incredible power, enormous potential, and more strength than we would believe possible, and the time to start trusting that Inner Power is now. Are you prepared to make these necessary changes now?

Appreciating and Loving Yourself

Once we realize that we have been puppets controlled by others, by environment, and by memories, we set out to free ourselves, to become our own person. We eventually reach that stage of awareness where we recognize anyone who tries to take control of our lives. This is a big step in our growth. When we first start to take control of our own lives, we might feel as though we are being selfish. It is not selfishness, but a guilt that tries to surface to get us to conform. Just hold your ground and stay in control of you.

The next step is the realization that now that you are in control, you have absolute freedom for the first time in your life. To maintain this freedom, you will want to direct yourself to that which you know to be right, and in your new awareness, you will tend to help others to discover themselves, too. After a while of being free, we come to appreciate that we have been given the choice to do anything. *I choose to turn my ego over to the navigating power that I call my Spiritual Essence to direct my life, knowing confidently that IT is better equipped to handle it than I. Thus, I fulfill my part in life, to let It's will be done on earth, through me.*

As we realize some of these spiritual truths, it becomes necessary to accept them as real for ourselves, not as an ego trip, but rather as a truth to be lived, internalized, and experienced. I encourage you to experience this for yourself. I'll show you how I experience it; then it's up to you as to how you interpret or express it.

How do I love myself? Let me count the ways.

Knowing that I and all else are a part of the ALL that is, removes the feeling of separation and shows that I am no greater and no lesser than anyone else. This one awareness disperses the need to be vain, conceited, or egotistical. I can therefore function freely to express the real me as I come to understand myself more fully.

I love myself for my preciousness, because I've become aware, in depth, that the Spiritual Essence is in me and flows through me.

I love myself for the appreciation that I feel for everything: the enjoyment, wonder, and awe of a beautiful sunset, the Inner calm and strength of recognizing love and hatred as the same emotion, and the excitement of knowing how to choose the former. Being in awe of the Universal Power and discovering myself as being part of this Creative Force is very thrilling.

I love myself for the love I feel and express to everyone whether they appear to deserve it or not.

I love myself because I want to follow my Inner Guidance in every way that I can, and express this intelligence in every action or thought.

I love the fact that I'm open to change, easy to talk with, an easygoing person, and no longer a weak one.

I love that I am strong enough to laugh, aware enough to enjoy every moment, and know that even though some of those moments may not seem pleasant, they are for my growth.

I love being me.

I love loving you.

I love love. There is no substitute. It can overcome anything. No matter how big the problem, loving can overcome it.

I love the whole of me that recognizes this.

I love that I can be entirely vulnerable, and consequently, invulnerable.

I love the fact that I love and that I am that Love personified. This enables me to love the Love in you, even though we may not have met.

I love that I can be true to myself first, foremost and always, with love, compassion, understanding, and consideration for others, and that no matter what I may have done or when it took place, I can forgive myself, really forgive myself, and try not to repeat the same mistake again. This awareness makes it easy for me to forgive others, too.

I love that my Spiritual Power just says *yes* to everything, and that I have the freedom to choose what I want. Having exposed myself to you, I now offer you the opportunity to use this exercise so that you may experience how to love. Start a complete list of your beauty. It's your Creator's gift to you, therefore it needs to be appreciated. Do it now.

Love and Romance

Are you happy? Think about that for a few moments. If the answer is no, do you know why? What can you do to change that? A magic wand would be nice. Love is a powerful emotion that leads to happiness or despair. It seems like a teeter-totter, with love on one side and hate on the other, with various degrees of both toward the middle. "Oh, if only I could change her or him, life would be so different." Love is probably the most important, yet least understood, word in the dictionary, and more than anything else, it plays a profound role in our lives. If we can understand what love is, we can be healthy and happy.

What is love? It's a kiss, a hug, . . . but I'm doing your work. Please take the time right now to make a list of, "What is love?" It's important to make a long list. I doubt that anyone can pin down what love is, for it's always so much more.

First, we need to acknowledge that there are many different types of love. There is the love of a parent for a child. Then there is the love of a child for its parents and grandparents, also its brothers and sisters. There is the eros love, the sweetheart love, sometimes called fascination; agape love, the love of the Spiritual Essence, one's belief system; the love of country, the motherland or fatherland; sexual, erotic love, or platonic love; nonsexual love for friends or society; scenic love, and love of animals. Please make your own list *now*.

Then there's liking, a degree less than loving. Sometimes we say things like, "I love sports, gardening, my work and my car." Statistics show that today in the U.S.A., sixty percent of the marriages end in divorce. With all that pain telling us to take a deeper look, it behooves us to do so. Let's start by looking at some of our mistaken beliefs about romantic love. It used to be that Hollywood would show a boy meeting a girl; then they fall in love and live happily ever after. Occasionally this does happen, of course, but obviously it's not the norm. One big problem is that we set ourselves up for a fall by being dishonest. I offer this observation as a discernment, an awareness of what transpires, without judgment. We lie to our friends, and often to ourselves, by pretending to be what we are not. It's known as trying to make an impression.

If a partner buys the impression, he or she comes to realize that he's bought an act or an illusion. The you that you've hidden can't stay buried forever, and if your partner fools you the same way, when the veneer wears thin, you may realize that you're strangers. One guideline is to be extremely honest and seek that as a requirement of your partner. Next, take time to examine your motives for a relationship. Is it because of loneliness, an unhappy home life, for financial support, or to escape from a situation? Is it primarily for sex, for challenge, for ego, to prove that you can get them, for hero worship for any reason, out of rebounding from another relationship or marriage, or from need, greed, selfishness, or prestige? Is your motive to make someone else jealous, to hurt them, to get what I can for me, myself and I, to own someone, to have a baby before I'm too old, or because we have a lot in common (s/he's my friend and I'd like to be with him/her)? No doubt there are many motives. Think about them.

One of the pitfalls to be aware of is needing someone else to make you happy. What sometimes happens is that we feel insufficient in ourselves, so we find someone else who needs us, and that compounds the problem. Subtleties can make a big difference. Wanting someone is fine. Needing someone could be a weakness to examine.

We've been taught to love. That's another trap we fall into. What's understood is, "I'll do this for you so that you'll do that for me." It's usually dishonest or manipulative. Love needs to be given unconditionally, i.e., no strings attached, no ulterior motives, just plain honest giving. A pure motive. The results are usually that you get love back in return, and that's a bonus, for your motive is pure giving, with no expectations. Learning how to love unconditionally will change your life so that you will wonder how you could possibly have lived any other way. It takes work and practice, touching many different aspects of life that may seem to have, individually, nothing to do with love. Yet, it's all a very necessary part of the package.

Part of loving unconditionally is to respect and encourage the fact that, although it is important to be united, it is essential to grow individually, too. You don't own your partner. Let them have their space to be who they are. Don't try and force them to live your script. View yourselves as free spirits, together.

This applies to children, too. They're not our children, even though we've been given the privilege to care for them. They're the "Property," Essence, or children of our Universal Power. Aside from a healthy discipline, they need their freedom to become what they want to be. We can't expect to live our lives through them. We may have wanted them to become a lawyer, but they may choose to become a carpenter. Wonderful, it's their choice. Sometimes parents wanted a son, but got a daughter, instead. They may have heaped their disappointment, regrets, and expectations on the child. This is hardly unconditional love, but it's not too late. Don't blame yourself with guilt, just see it as a mistake, and choose to start changing your old habits.

Expanding Love

Love to be honest with yourself and others, and develop the principles of love. Have the honesty to refuse to bribe others or be bribed by them and live by the Golden Rule. Knowing these principles is not sufficient. They have to be lived.

As we grow, we will come to give thanks for this wisdom. I know that I make mistakes, but I also know that there is within me a spiritual perfection, and as I follow that spiritual perfection, or intuition, I am guided for the benefit of all, especially myself.

As I expand my awareness, I give thanks that I can be:

Happy enough to smile,

Strong and honest enough to cry,

Tough enough to stick with upright principles even if others
    think I'm a dreamer,

Gentle enough to care,

Aware enough to be interested,

Empathetic enough to listen and really hear,

Trustworthy enough to keep confidentiality, and

Courageous enough to love not only those who love me but to

Realize the wisdom that only love conquers hate.

I give thanks that I'm humble enough to forgive and aware enough that forgiveness is more for my benefit than for the one I'm forgiving.

I know that making friends of enemies is a challenge well rewarded. I give thanks and love the beauty within me, as well as your indwelling beauty, and I am grateful to have the knowledge that as a unique individual, I can love and treat myself with the same respect that I show you, for I am no more important and no less an individual than you are.

I give thanks for life, laughter, happiness, and tears, as they are all part of the web of life. So often it has been my pain that has brought my joy, and vice versa.

I give thanks that I love you, and that I love me, also.

Destination of Love

A baby of innocence, a Gift of great Love,
Born in a world that's forgotten.
How will it grow, what will it know?
And how will it be taught here?
To be first, number one, or carry a gun,
It's me versus you, don't you know.
Getting's the goal and getting it now,
It doesn't seem to matter much how.
But that journey gets tougher and leaves us much rougher,
Escaping in drugs or in booze.
Could it be that we're setting ourselves up to lose?
Others, it seems, had different dreams,
And flowed more with life from the start.
They, too, had their struggles and setbacks in life,
For how else could they grow?
Accepting and moving on, somehow they seemed to know that
Learning's the name, and life's the game.
To discover our egos and then, gently let them go.
Our uniqueness is special,
Yet, we are really the same,
Another experience of illusion in life's paradox game,
So that we may learn from separation, to part,
Embracing love, understanding, and wisdom with
        a Unified Heart.

CHAPTER TWELVE

To Everything a Season

New Year

HERE ARE SOME THOUGHTS on the New Year. As we let the New Year in, with a fond farewell we also let go of the old one and make a fresh start. It is said that today is the first day of the rest of your life. Wonderful. And just what are we going to do with our todays? Just as the New Year offers promise, each day offers us the opportunity to create it into a special day. Many people who are seriously ill belong to a group called, "Make Today Count." And they do. They appreciate each day as it comes along and count their blessings. There's no room for negativity in their minds. They're a real inspiration for those of us who are blessed with good health.

Getting out of bed on the right side with a sunny smile and the personality to match is a great way to start the day. Looking for the good in everything and everybody, offering them encouragement, and caring about them is a divine experience. When we give of ourselves, we give it all, and it tends to return to us. Just like smiles, you can never outgive them. If this year is to be our happiest so far, it has to start with a positive attitude. And guess who's in charge of that. Right, you are. If you are not entirely happy the way you are, create the circumstance that will make you happy.

Make the changes that feel right for you. Do things differently, and sometimes that means getting out of your comfort zone to grow to where you need to be. Some of us have been dead for years; we've just not laid down. Come to life. Claim your divine inheritance. Be in your thoughts, actions, and deeds, the child of the Universal Power that you are. The true you is magnificent.

To help bring out some of the beauties of life, you might try and capture some of these attitudes. If you haven't got them, learn them: Think of your Universal Power, light, love, preciousness, joy, and abundance. Be in the knowing stage.

Be aware, alert, happy, vibrant, alive, content, positive. Have fun. Be appreciative, giving and receiving.

Be open, honest and trustworthy, dependable, available and constructive, committed, gently strong, caring, empathetic, interested, sincere.

Be interesting. Be a speaker *and* a listener.

Be non-judgmental, calm, pleasant, loving, and open.

Be giving and understanding, while being true to yourself and others.

Be objective. Share good will. Use your Inner Intelligence. Have a calm strength. Be cooperative, concerned, and *listen.* Be in the moment, thoughtful. Be kind, confident, free and open-minded. Have a sense of humor. Be easy going.

Be decisive, courageous, worthy, responsible, reliable, respectable, reasonable, patient, supportive, warm, and flexible, and come from a place of integrity. Love is strong, yet gentle.

Be empathetic, firm, and kind, and go into action.

Appreciation

Early one morning I was sitting reading a book, and as I looked up to reflect on it for a moment, my eyes were drawn to the profusion of colors of my neighbor's beautiful roses, and to our own little garden of comparable beauty. The sun was just up and shining brightly. Thanksgiving was a few weeks away, but for me it was right *now*, as gratitude welled up within me to appreciate my eyesight, one of the free gifts of our magnificent bodies that we tend to take so much for granted (unless it's threatened).

As I sat contemplating the marvel of this incredible machine (my body), I became more and more aware of its miraculous functions. I invite you to take a moment right now to think about yourself, and to count your blessings. The more we look for our good each day, the more our lives change and reflect it, and Thanksgiving becomes a daily pleasure rather than only an annual event. This is true of the Christmas season, too, as a celebration of life. I choose to celebrate life every day, for each day is a brand new one to be lived, experienced, and blessed as *today*. As the blessings of *this* day abound, I feel good will towards all humankind and start living accordingly.

Aging

Who said that the second half is best? This suggests comparison with the first half. Many of us start in, full of enthusiasm, with goals to achieve entailing study, hard work, and some accomplishments and disappointments. Often we rear a family, which requires time, attention, and understanding. We might briefly say that the first half of our lives are spent very industriously, busily and competitively trying to accumulate wealth, property, cars, and all sorts of material things. For some, these dreams have materialized, but for others, perhaps they did not attain their goals—or came to have different ones. Nevertheless, a time finally arrives when we choose to retire, or are forced to retire physically, or due to our *age* or a host of other reasons.

After working all our lives, how do we feel about this? There are probably as many different answers as there are retired people. Frequently for the first month or two, it's great to have all the freedom to rest and do nothing but putter, play golf or travel. But then very often the feeling may creep in, *what's next,* or, *this tends to get boring.* Some feel, *my children have grown and left; of what use am I any more?* Still others worry about illness and, paramount, they fear death.

The second half is the best!? It doesn't sound like it, but then let's examine other possibilities. For some, unquestionably the second half is the best, for others it isn't. What makes the difference? Most of us have not prepared ourselves for these latter years, and the results are a hit or miss hodgepodge of experiences. As we may have finally learned in the first half, what makes a big difference in the way we live our lives is our *attitude*. Funny thing, attitude—we can either develop it from our experiences, or have our attitude govern our experiences. We can decide to fight our aging process by pretending to ourselves that we're still only forty years of age and live the losing and frustrating battle of trying to do the things we no longer can, or try living in the past glories of what we were, what we used to do, or what we used to own—the *yesterdays!* Then there are the tomorrows, with all the uncertainties and concerns with the *what ifs?* and, ultimately, death itself.

Let's first take an honest look at ourselves and realize that we have the opportunity to embrace change and make it work for us today. Stop living in *yesterday* or *tomorrow* and start appreciating *today*. Make each day count. As second-halfers, we are privileged to have the time (out of the rat race), to reflect on where we've been, and to see where we're going. Obviously, the purpose of life does not mean for us to work until we retire, and then with many *good years* still ahead, to *die off*. As we look at nature, we find that everything is *in place,* coordinated perfectly, and in harmony—everything except man, that is!

Could it be possible that our second half is the bonus in life that enables us to learn harmony and happiness with the rest of nature? Jerome Ellison, in his book *Life's Second Half: The Pleasures of Aging*, indicates ways in which we may discover new dimensions in our lives, making them meaningful and creative. He states, "If you're going to have a social life, why have one based on small talk? Why not have a social life based on large talk?" Large talk, I consider, means delving into the who, how, where, and what we are all about, our relationship to the cosmos. This can be deepened through discussion, reading, and experiencing life's purpose for us.

When we're living our *second half*, let's do a good job of it, rather than a sloppy one. To do this we need to unlearn some of our *tribal habits*, beliefs, and fears, and the greatest of these is usually death, even though all religions, sages, and wise men point out that life is not just a body, but continues after death.

What is this life Essence that keeps our hearts beating while we are still in the physical body? We can discover this life and start living here and now, seeking ways of expansion. We have no need to compete with our former youth—give way to wisdom. There's a lot of truth in the saying, "We get old too soon and smart too late." It's not too late—now is the time! By stretching our minds and imaginations, we can discover so much about outer and inner space—so many miracles waiting to be uncovered, new goals to be thought of and talked about, and new values to be introduced, all with harmonious overtones instead of greedy motives. We have much to pass on to our young people, for a better world and for our children and grandchildren to benefit from. Meditation, a spiritual approach, group discussion, and love are some of the solutions.

Heart's Music

We are all put here to discover our heart's music, to let it flow through us, primarily for our delight, and also for the benefit of others who may wish to hear.

We were each given our own music, and each drummer was different, but it was the tune that we were meant to follow in the best way that we knew how, and it was all necessary for us to experience before returning Home.

Attach no judgment to your life; in the Big picture we each did just what we did. Our errors were for us and others to learn from. The good and the bad, our failures and our successes, were all just labels we gave to experiences, for in reality, we are all just part of life's orchestra.

Death

Death is a subject that few people like to talk about. Society has *brought us up* to come from a *fear understanding*. I encourage *faith* and *knowing* understanding. Our conflict in understanding stems from the fact that we are both spiritual and physical beings. Our spiritual side *never* dies, only our physical. When we understand this, we can welcome death as a graduation to a higher plateau of understanding. That does not mean that we do not feel grief when a loved one dies, but that pain is for *our* temporary loss—until our feelings adjust to the realization that the person has graduated. If we could see the *picture of life* in a big enough way, we'd know that all's okay.

*Again on Death**

This article on death could change your life, for the better, yet it's a subject that many people like to sweep under the rug and forget about. The problem is that they don't forget, but secretly worry about it. Is there another approach we could take?

Do you remember as a child, the illusion of Santa Claus, how he was on every street corner—and yet it was a hoax? Death, too, is a hoax. It is not an end, but rather a beginning. Our problem has been that we believe we are our body, because like Santa Claus, we've seen it around. We are our body, but so much more than that, too. We are part of the Spiritual Essence of God.

We're actually spiritual *beings* dressed in physical bodies, and when we die we merely discard our physical bodies, as the butterfly does when it leaves its cocoon.

By opening our minds to this understanding, we can view our lives as different aspects of growing. Life is constantly changing. We change physically and mentally, and when the time is ripe for us, we move on to a higher plane of understanding. Spiritually, we live forever.

---

*This article is courtesy of the Teleos Institute (Love Project) from their book, *The Love Project Way,* by Arleen Lorrance and Diane Kennedy Pike.

The Death of a Loved One

Many experiences occur during our lives. It is not necessarily the experience that is frightening or devastating, but the way in which we handle it.

Choice is a life process, and we can guide our thinking and subsequent actions, allowing the energy to flow, instead of short-circuiting it. As a result of learning and living the Love Project principles,* I've found myself constantly growing in my ability to cope with life. To me, life is a class of experiences to be discovered, worked with, and understood until we begin to realize what could be another Love Project principal: Everything's okay. Usually, if we grow a lot it's from a particularly big problem, for problems are opportunities.

Many years ago, my wife, who had been extremely healthy, developed (through a chain of *circumstances*), terminal cancer. Fortunately, I believe that we are all Spirit, Energy, and that life is just temporarily personified in the form of a particular *person,* and that *death* is just a moving forward to another classroom of experiences. My belief was to be put to the test when, after two years of illness, my wife died. What were my thoughts, feelings, and plans when, after nearly thirty years of marriage, I was alone? I had many and varied feelings. I felt appreciation that the Creator had chosen to call her home when It did, so that she did not linger on, suffering. I felt a deep void, for, particularly in the last months, as she'd of necessity come to depend on me physically more and more, we'd become closer than ever before. Now she was *gone.*

I cried many tears, those that I could not shed in front of her, and those that I felt for the future lifetime we would miss having together. A particular love song on the radio would start me off, or a phone call from someone who hadn't heard, or uncancelled mail subscriptions in her name. As I let the tears flood out, I was aware that I was crying for myself—my loneliness, my hurt. Deep inside of me I was grateful that she was no longer suffering, and I knew, "All is well for her now," that she'd moved on toward a higher plateau of growth.

---

* See "Love Project" Principles, p. 73.

We have innumerable choices. Thus I looked at myself as an observer and viewed the many alternatives open to me. I could keep crying or pull myself (through running down my health) into a disease. I could also stand in the corner and pout, damning, with a *why me?* attitude.

Create your own reality and be the change you want to see happen, were principles that stuck out in my mind. Don't spend weeks on mind trips or what if's. I told myself to *just do it.* So it was that just a few weeks after I'd buried my wife, I decided to be the person I want to be, happy, loving, caring, and sharing, starting from just where I was.

I embarked on a merry-go-round of meetings for personal growth, self-discovery, and the study of comparative religions, to discover that all paths lead to the same Universal Power and that we all are one. There is a unity in the diversity of life. With this discovery, I was able, finally, to understand how to:

Receive all people as beautiful exactly where they are, a principle I'd struggled with for years. New doors opened, strangers became friends, a new life emerged, I found that I could be alone, and, whereas it is nice to have friends, I no longer had to have them. I could survive with or without them.

The mysteries of life started to unfold for me and a new, awesome, and exciting world of understanding began to make life more and more worthwhile for me. I give thanks for the blessings I have, appreciating our Spiritual Nature, which reminds me of the truth of who I really am, and as the fog clears, I see more and more of my Spiritual Nature.

CHAPTER THIRTEEN

Social Change

Common Sense

OUR WHOLE CONCEPT OF LIFE needs overhauling. What happens when there is a war is that two opposing nations struggle to kill one another in order to gain or protect their land. Allies take sides, and soon we have many nations fighting many nations. Eventually, after thousands of people have been separated, severely mutilated, or killed, we have to find a way to stop. And so, some sort of agreement is made, and the war is finally over. It's very hard to stop a war. Each side is bent on winning, so there's no communication, except usually from a third party trying to mediate. But each fighting nation has its pride and doesn't want to lose, and that costs lives.

If we have the brains and the talent to negotiate a peace settlement under extreme conditions of war, surely those same brains and talent could prevent one while the lines of communication are still open, without all the painful physical and mental agony of war. How can we prevent these wars from occurring? The answer is, by the way we think and then act. Let me illustrate what could happen.

Throughout the world, mothers are giving birth to babies and then bringing them up the best way they can, feeding them, loving them, looking after them, and sitting up with them all night when they are sick. Until recently, this was considered the mother's job; men were usually being too macho or busy and concerned with their job to spend enough time with the family, so that they did not get as close in feelings for the children as the mother did. Fortunately, that's now changing as men begin to realize what they've been missing and are allowing themselves to mature with their feelings. These parents love their children. Those children are precious, and indeed their life is precious, and that's what we need to concentrate our thinking on. Did you bring your children into the world to become killing machines? Do you want your child torturing, mutilating, or killing other people, destroying their lives, property, hopes, and dreams, or have your child and family suffering these same consequences?

When the military might is shown on television going *out there* to protect us, we often allow ourselves to be duped into thinking, patriotically, *how wonderful.* But think deeper about the consequences, the agony that awaits. Don't let children die for their country anymore. Have them live for it. I'm not being ungrateful, unsympathetic, or criticizing the wonderful people who died or fought in wars past. That seemed the only way that we knew, then, but we are now learning that we have alternative approaches available. We need to use our massive intelligence and the best brains available to seek peaceful solutions, and that requires people with mature minds, highly trained in conflict resolution, clearly thinking in terms of humanity, love, compassion, and concern with life and with each precious person, everywhere. Life is a gift to us. Who would want to snuff it out?

Proposed Humanities Program

Our country has been quite divided on the abortion issue, but little has been said about preventing pregnancy in the first place. It seems to me that many of our problems could be lessened if we embarked upon a massive, mature, educational program aimed in many directions simultaneously.

We require a humanities program that will teach us how to get along with our relatives and with one another. This will teach and demonstrate the advantages of working constructively together, using conflict resolution as a method to talk things out rather than becoming aggressive and hostile. This will help to resolve our differences and develop a caring attitude rather than an "I don't care" attitude.

Conventional education is important, but our society reflects the broken homes, hurts, hates, disfigurements, and unhappiness caused through drinking, drugs, and other escapes, which derive from not knowing how to cope with life. It is essential for us to concentrate on our attitudes and learn how to get them to work for us, rather than allow them to destroy us.

Therefore, let us start constructive attitude classes with kindergartners and progress through all grades. I am aware that some of this has already begun, but it also needs to be emphasized and re-emphasized as the children grow.

Here are some suggestion for the curriculum.

1) Ask the children to create a list of things they do not like in people. Have them really stretch to make a long list, and then add additional negative descriptions. Next have them mark any of those attitudes that they personally practice. (See Appendix B.)

2) Next, ask the children to make a long list of traits that they like about their friends. Have them really think and keep expanding the list. Then have them mark any of these attitudes that they practice. Share that to have a friend, we need to *BE* a friend. See if they would want to trade any of their negative attitudes for positive attitudes, and ask why.

Do not put the children down for their negative attitudes, but explain that this is a learning situation. To have a happier life, one needs to learn to let go of the negative attitudes, while expanding on the positive attitudes, because we all want to be happier. Get them to picture how it would feel if the whole class were to adopt positive attitudes. (See Appendix A.)

Have children role play both attitudes. Discuss why positive attitudes are preferable. Assist in showing them how they can let go of negative attitudes. For example, explain how they can transform hostility or anger into using that energy for something constructive, such as taking a walk or a run, cleaning their room, listening to enjoyable music, or reading something that interests them.

We also need a sexual program that will include the pros, cons, and responsibilities of the boy as well as the girl, both in regards to sexual experiences and should pregnancy occur, a program which explains how drugs, alcohol, cigarettes, and behavior affect the baby greatly while still in the womb.

Most of us have come from dysfunctional homes and will perpetuate and repeat the same dysfunctions in our own homes, unless we adopt a more constructive method of parent training as an important priority.

Sexual Program (starting at about seven years of age):

Be relaxed. Children are less tense than are most adults, and they feel that as a barrier. Get yourself comfortable in being able to talk about sex. Assume that most parents have not adequately done this, so you are the teacher. What are the essentials to be conveyed and discussed? Become able to talk about a penis or a vagina as comfortably as you would talk about an arm or a leg, or any part of the anatomy.

With regard to attitudes, some children may have been molested and carry great pain or guilt in this connection. If this is noticed, they definitely need professional help and counselling. Some may have gay or homosexual tendencies, and one needs to be very sensitive, open, caring, and understanding in this case. You might want to examine your own attitude in this connection so as not to cause the child any problems if you happen to be biased. It is better to disqualify yourself and have someone unbiased teach the class if this is the case.

Demonstrate a healthy attitude. Sex is joyful, and as adults, we should not carry any guilt of its being dirty, animalistic, or something to be tolerated. A distinction needs to be made between having sex and making love. Sex can imply self-gratification for many wrong reasons, with little or no concern for the partner. Making love, on the other hand, suggests caring, gentleness, consideration, and interest in mutual satisfaction, whether or not it includes the sexual act.

Discussion about sex should, of course, include the male and female reproductive organs, and what happens when sex occurs. The reasons for birth control, and the fact that none are one hundred percent safe, and that condoms are not necessarily effective in preventing AIDS due to the possibility that the AIDS virus is so small that it may penetrate through a condom. Condoms are safer than not using them, and they may prevent other sexual diseases or pregnancy. Before having sex, young people need to be reminded of how many unwanted pregnancies occur, and of how essential it is to be aware of this. Questions to ask themselves might include, "Am I aware that this could happen to me, that I too could get pregnant? Are my 'feelings' the only reason for seeking sex?"

What other reasons may be involved? As a young man, am I manipulating the girl to have sex with me? Am I being honest? Am I prepared to support (for 18 years) a child that I might accidentally father? What would working to support this baby do to my college education? Am I aware of the responsibilities of raising a child, of the lack of freedom to go out frequently. For example, instead, I may be staying awake half the night looking after a hungry, crying baby. Am I ready to sacrifice my youth and settle down as head of a family, with all that this entails? Is perhaps the price of a few minutes of fun too high a price to pay?

President Clinton has promised that fathers will pay for their child support and not get away with it anymore. Be aware that this is not a game. It is mighty important to you. Also of prime importance is to realize that our children are not our possessions to be treated as objects. They are children of a Universal Power, to be treated with the greatest respect, appreciation, and love. This realization alone may greatly help in the prevention of psychological, mental, physical, and sexual abuse of all kinds.

Parents should be educated and required to encourage their children to build their self-esteem, not tear them down with negative statements of how no-good they are. We have learned to judge people by what they do. If their actions are bad, we call them *bad people*. The new constructive approach is to separate the person from their action, by discerning instead of judging. It works like this: we see the person as a good person, but their behavior is not acceptable. Instead of getting caught up with personality blaming, such as, "You are no good, you are untidy," say, "I care about you, but I cannot accept your untidiness."

Another reason that parents don't often praise their children is because they themselves have been brought up in a negative way and consequently have a low self-esteem. They have been taught only how to punish, rather than to be encouraging.

Here are a few pointers in teaching or in improving your own self-esteem:

You are a child of our Spiritual Nature. You are unique, and there is no one anywhere in the world exactly like you. You are special. Each one of us is special. You are precious and house incredible potential gifts that you have been afraid to share in case of being "put down" as being stupid. We need to have confidence in our own ability. We need to question whether other people's opinions, when they say something cannot be done, are accurate. Learn to trust yourself and your hunches, and be open-minded. Usually we are much more talented than we believe. Do not compare yourself with others. Compete only with yourself, and persist in being the best you that you can be. Be gentle with yourself. You are no more important than anyone else, and neither are you *less* important than anyone else. Have and develop a healthy attitude about yourself. You are okay. Develop common sense, and rely more on your hunches. Not everything is *logical*. Feelings, emotions, circumstances, and beliefs play a big part in our decisions.

One of our goals in growing is to recognize our value. We are not second rate citizens. In a non-egotistical way, we are very important. Be yourself, not a carbon copy of someone else. Appreciate your uniqueness. As we gain in this understanding, we learn to become assertive, and herein lies a potential trap. We may become so assertive that we go right past becoming assertive and become aggressive. When becoming independent or assertive, it is essential to bring with it more love—not less! Real strength does not have to prove anything.

Think of your positive and pleasant friends and people that you know. What traits or habits do they have that appeal to you? Chances are that those assets would also work for you. (Please see Appendix A.)

SECTION THREE
On Religion and Beliefs

About Religion

Isn't it ironic that the one aspect of life that should join us together has been the very aspect that has frequently separated us? Fortunately, religious leaders are getting together to understand that although there are differences in religious beliefs, we need to be tolerant of them and condone rather than condemn them.

It is my belief that one of the common denominators of most religions is love, which happens to be what this book is all about. By sharing unconditional love from my viewpoint, I hope to encourage harmony and unity, to expand your application of love in and perhaps for your own religion so that you live or come to live the essence of your teaching even more fully and joyfully.

I ask that you discern my intent rather than sit in judgment; however, the decision is yours. I do not ask you to buy into my ideas. I just offer them as spiritual hors d'oeuvres to take what you want. You can accept none of it, part of it, or go for the whole dinner—bon apetit.

This is a section of spiritual essays, thoughts, insights and beliefs to help stimulate *Big Talk* instead of *Small Talk* amongst relatives and friends. Facilitating is easy if you read a chapterette, ponder it, and then discuss pros and cons with your viewpoints and suggestions. Please keep comments constructive.

CHAPTER FOURTEEN

The Spiritual Nature

Inspirations

MY FOREMOST PRIVILEGE or task is to share methods or principles that create peace. Whereas I believe that all religions share truths and important guidelines to live by, I am not here to favor any one of them. What religion one follows or does not follow is up to the individual's particular belief, just as my belief system is between my Universal Power and me. If we believe in freedom we all agree that this wise part of the U.S. Constitution is an essential step toward peace and freedom. I am referring to one's privilege to worship according to their beliefs and the opportunity for each of us to express our freedom of choice in our belief system. That, for me, is the meaning of what "One nation under God" is all about.

I believe that Jesus, Buddha, and others went beyond the dogmas of religions and just lived their principles. My lesson as an individual is to be my highest and best self, based on those principles, seeking, as they did, my innermost guidance and testing its validity by seeing that it fits the principles of love and compassion. Surely this can only bring peace. Love of a Universal Essence is our common denominator, even if it's known by many titles. I choose to live my life by sharing that unconditional love, and submit that as more people do that, we will come closer to peace.

By studying comparative religions I've come to see the beauty in each of them, and I've come to know that living principles of unconditional love can only enhance each of the religions and not deplete them.

I believe that the Spirit of God that is called by countless Divine religious names, is One all-inclusive, all-encompassing God.

To emphasize our inclusiveness, I use words such as: our Spiritual Power, Spiritual Nature, Spiritual Self, Spiritual Inner Guidance, Spiritual Source or Creator, (Spiritual) Essence, Higher Consciousness, Ultimate Source, Universal Power, Universal Nature, the Energy Force, the Eternal, and very respectfully, It.

These words refer to the All-Knowing Timeless Spiritual Source that has always been, that I call God. Please remember to use the Divine name of your belief.

I believe that our Spiritual Nature is not a vengeful God—but rather a caring and supportive power of love, and that we are that *LOVE* personified (we are made of this Spiritual Essence). I believe that we are unique, and that we are created of this Universal Spirit. Let in the light to disperse the clouds that hide your *true* identity from yourself. To really appreciate *Peace* is to dare to believe that you already possess that Spiritual Power, and that by flowing with that Intelligence you live from the Eternal center of love, and not only glow and become a light in your own life, but also in the lives of others.

The spirit of our Universal Source is everywhere and as we seek it, we will discover that It already *is* what we are. As we contemplate love in all things and express this love to others on a daily basis, we begin to flow with life rather than struggle against it.

My endeavors are to expand all areas of understanding, to bridge the gap between religions, concentrating on their similarities rather than their differences, and to extract the spiritual essence from each of them. I believe that all religions have truths that, if learned and applied, are beneficial to our health and happiness. However, knowledge of these truths without their understanding or application are of little benefit. I offer individual formulas, guidance, and instruction to achieve these ends. I feel that all religions can, like the spokes of a wheel, lead to the *central hub of Life*, the Source of all.

I caution that fear teachings, designed to hold onto congregations, hold us back. Religion could be like a parent whose aim is to teach it's child independence, and when that is done, to step into the background, enjoying the results and being available only if needed.

I believe that taught religion is but a practical stepping stone to self-awareness. Religions should be spiritual in their focus, their formulas guiding one gently to the discovery that the Spiritual Nature is within each of us, and, once this is properly understood, that we draw on the intuition of that Inner Essence of undistorted *TRUTH* for our future guidance.

The one thing common to man, animal, plant, and substance is our Source of Everything, Nature, the Universal Power, the Creative Spiritual Essence. As we become more aware of this, there develops a greater tolerance for other's viewpoints, and an understanding and unity among the diversities of life emerges, with a constructive desire to work things out with an Ultimate Awareness.

Understanding these benefits and principles has worked in my life, and I've seen them working in the lives of others. I now find myself not merely interested, but impelled, propelled, and compelled to share these gifts with others who are inclined to receive them. It is my ardent hope that you will be inspired to reach your highest potential, your Inner Love, for *You* truly are precious.

Do I Belive in God?

This question may be one you have asked yourself, without finding a satisfactory answer. Perhaps one of the reasons for this is that the various religions seem conflicting, or it may be you have been disillusioned by the actions of a religious person.

Sometimes the dogmas are hard to take, others may seem boring. Perhaps your experience has been finding yourself in desperation, turning to prayer, and because that didn't seem to work, you have given up believing.

As I see religion, its intentions are good, but seemingly inadequate. One thing does stand out. They all seem to point to basic truths.

The next step is how to apply these truths in our daily lives, to get a clear picture of what or who God is, and ask does this Spiritual Power exist?

In my opinion, It is not a separate person somewhere out there in the sky. The Bible indicates we are made in His image, tending to give the logical impression that it is a man or woman, as we are. So we are apt to believe Him to be a magical person.

It seems to me that, "We are made in His image," means we are made of the same material stuff, matter, or more accurately, spirit, which for lack of a better word, I will call Energy, or Spiritual Power.

Science has proven that even in steel, which appears solid, there is enormous activity in the form of electrons, neutrons, and atoms. In essence, although steel seems solid, it contains unseen movement or life within it.

This Energy is the Supreme and Eternal Spirit that is in *everything* and *everybody*. It takes on different forms (manifestation), but is still the ALL. It is suppressed in humans, until our discovery of It. We are all drops of that Holy Ocean.

The fact is we already are spiritually *perfect*. The problem is we don't believe it. There really is nothing to do other than come to this realization, for as we concentrate on the Universal Power as the Source, It reveals the truth. It is the Inner Self that illumines the man or woman, who then receives and understands Love and Truth intuitively.

As this occurs, we learn that there is nothing we have to prove, and we start automatically becoming a wiser person, choosing to express the good as we come to know it, rather than fighting the bad or trying to prove how right we are. We just *are*, and our personal discovery of more wisdom leads us ever forward in the direction of Love and Harmony, almost automatically.

I invite you to pause for a few moments to reflect on this first chapterette before going on to the next one.

From Error to Fulfillment

There has to be more to life than working, eating, sleeping, and TV. Usually to get information we ask: who, what, when, why and where. Let's start with what.

What is the purpose of life?

In very simple terms, "To discover who we really are."

How do we do this?

First we need some background or understanding. Next, we need the interest to seek it, then the working tools for discovery.

Since we are dealing with what appears to be unknown, we need to use something we are already familiar with to try to grasp what appears to be the incomprehensible, as for example, electricity.

What is electricity?

Electricity is a force which has always been available, but which was only discovered about one hundred years ago. What does electricity do? What is its function? When properly applied, electricity is a wonder of the world that we just take for granted. It can illuminate and propel just about everything.

However, when there is an overload or burnout, everything stops—freezers, refrigerators, elevators, computers, traffic lights, even gas pumps. Everything comes to a stop. Chaos! And only then do we appreciate what we've taken for granted.

Also, the same electricity that brings us the wonders and comforts, if improperly applied, can give us painful shocks, or even kill us. So it is necessary for us to be aware of this Power, and to use it in a right and safe manner.

The main points are:

1) Electricity has always existed.

2) It became available to us only when we discovered it.

3) We can use its power for good or harm. It's available to us, and we can use it or not.

4) It has a negative and a positive, opposites, a dichotomy.

Let's examine how this example applies to humans and what we can learn from it to improve our lives. What is man/woman? Man is a confused being, in conflict with himself and others, seeking harmony but missing the understanding or the self-discipline to attain it.

We are an energy force, each of us capable of positive (good) or negative (harm). When we understand how this works, we can choose to behave in a positive or negative mode.

Until we understand, we are like a teeter-totter of positive and negative emotions, love and hate, good intentions—poor results! We have only to look at the world to see how negative our thinking and consequent actions have been to warrant such results.

But take heart. Much good has also been achieved, and there is a solution. *You're it.* Here's how it works. In each of us is the Universal Power to use in a positive or negative way.

The Universal Power always says YES. If we choose the positive, we get positive results. If we choose negative, we get negative results. You can rely upon your Spiritual Power's YES, YES, YES, YES, YES! Like a camera, it takes the picture of what we're aiming at. It doesn't care what we're aiming at. When we click the switch, that's what we get. So, when we've made enough poor pictures (mistakes), we'll want to turn to better scenes.

The positive approach tends to be calm, yet very much alive: understanding, harmonious, caring, and loving in its highest form, unconditionally.

The negative approach is bullying, aggressive, conniving, deceptive, cunning, and an exciting mode. The deception is that the negative appears more attractive, exciting, and easier to do, but the results are disastrous.

The positive requires some self-discipline, and the results bring us from our dilemmas to understanding.

By our moods, we are aware of the conflict, but rather than choose the positive (good team within), we seem to favor giving our energy to the excitement and to cunning deception, using the energy negatively. Thus the good within us becomes dimmer.

Actually there is no positive or negative energy. There is just energy that we choose to use in a positive or negative way. It is the same energy.

When we realize we are One with our Spiritual Nature, we become aware that as co-creators, we are constantly creating something in our thoughts, which becomes materialized. If we don't know this, we just create whatever comes of Nature's Laws. Since we co-create, we can program what we create to be what we want. We have been given the freedom of choice to do this.

This law works for us constantly. It is impersonal. It produces what we think about and focus upon. The Spiritual Power loves us, but It doesn't care what we plant—It just grows it.

We experience our mistakes, and as we grow from them, we make fewer of them and continue along the pathway until we eventually realize our perfection.

Applying Nature's Laws in positive *Highest Good* ways for all concerned is a shortcut to this achievement and an easier route to travel—Yes!

Then why do we keep making the wrong choices? It's because we're *lazy*. In the beginning it appears to take effort to discipline ourselves, then, paradoxically, it becomes *effortless*. What we've been doing is rooting for the wrong team, and thereby getting the wrong results, for what we give power to, becomes manifested.

So why do we select the negative? It's because we're more familiar with our insecure security blanket than with daring to risk trusting an intangible, incomprehensible, Universal Power and taking responsibility for our actions. It seems easier to blame others.

We are deceived into believing that our personality is what we are, and this deludes us into thinking our ego knows it all, and that we need to be pompous, greedy or selfish, prideful, unforgiving, resentful, angry, revengeful, or full of hate, as ego controls us through our feelings, preying on our pride and other emotions, and controlling us through them.

In our ignorance, we have allowed our ego to control our lives. We have thought there were only two ways of handling this, either by

1) giving in to our feelings and emotions, a natural thing to do, or

2) trying desperately to maintain self-control, fighting ourselves not to give in to temptation, and either losing the battle, or being frustrated because its really what we wanted to do.

It's like you can't win. But there's another way—*effortlessly*, through understanding. Our feelings and emotions are natural and normal; everyone has them. We need them to be able to Love Unconditionally, yet we need to be in control of our negative feelings by gently transforming them, and not trying to force our will, but just letting it happen. This can be learned through the discipline of meditation.

What is meditation?

Meditation is a means of quieting the mind so that we allow our mind to *rest*. By so doing, we become more aware, and can, in our calmness, view things as an impersonal observer (just the opposite of being emotionally hysterical, when we might say and do things for which we are later sorry).

As we begin to view things unemotionally as an observer, we become in charge of them. As we see more clearly, we make more correct choices, because we choose to let the Spiritual Essence guide our actions. This Power, which is always there, becomes clearer for us to see as we learn how to stop blocking its flow (which we tend to do by keeping our minds busy with the misguided belief that constant thoughts, education, and review will eventually bring desired results). Getting thoughts out of our head requires us to be in the present moment, *not* yesterday or tomorrow, but today—*right now!*

By knowing the problems that we've experienced and by trying to remedy our mistakes, it becomes easier for us to recognize the struggle others have, thus making it easier for us to forgive them for their shortcomings, too.

It is essential that we examine our own mistakes and be sorry for them, then forgive ourselves, so we may stop feeling guilty (living in the past), and concentrate on living in today.

Learn to forgive everyone. Why? Because you're wanting to change. If the other person doesn't yet know any better, they may give you cause to need to forgive. This cause is good practice. As the prayer says, Forgive us our debts (sins), as we forgive our debtors. Make allowances for their behavior or misbehavior, and stand as a correctant for them, not by acting superior or by being a raving dictator at their level.

Therefore, here are some practical applications:

1) Forgive (immediately, right now, make allowances).

2) If you see a situation that requires correcting, do it in a *firm, kind* manner. Disagree if necessary, *but,* do *not* be disagreeable. Be patient, follow the Golden Rule.

3) If people are seeking, share your discovery, so the world may be a better place, and people become more and more *Human, Children of Peace.*

Make a start by listening within, thinking, and doing the things you wish to see happen. *Do it today. Do it every day.* With the Inner Power's guidance and trusting that wisdom, we grow in the right direction, gaining more energy, strength, understanding, and the wisdom of knowing. Our life encompasses the apparent duality of an earthly and a spiritual world. The earthly world seems to have us born into experiencing errors, inheriting the mistakes of past genera-tions, the teachings of which are pain, jealousy, hatred, revenge, disharmony of the world, violence, drugs, alcohol, murder, wars, and greed. Meanwhile, our life also houses the spiritual world of potential understanding, calm knowing, right action rather than reaction, peace, love, and joy.

In the formative years, we were subject to our parent's beliefs and society's molding of our individual uniqueness into carbon copies of one another. Hypnotized into robots, we tend to accept this way of life with some resistance, usually with rebellions and attempts of escape. Eventually we become aware that we have a choice in life, that we no longer have to be a victim, and that we can take charge of our lives.

As we reach this understanding, it becomes necessary that with this choice comes responsibility and the need for awareness. We live in a world of apparent duality, but actually our lives are to experi-ment with the options, and to learn that we can choose to continue in ignorance (with unsatisfactory results), or choose to live from our conscience. The choice is ours.

Let's suppose you have chosen the wise path, the path least travelled. Where do we start, how do we start? And, isn't it scary and risky? Actually, what is scary and risky is if we do not make the changes.

The changes begin when we realize that so far we've reacted to life with our personalities, which contained a big dose of ego, pride, and unforgiveness. This needs to be changed, and to do that requires us to want to rely on our Spiritual Nature. This is most effectively done through meditation, contemplation, and appreciation.

Pause and contemplate before proceeding.

Religion

I'd like to share some thoughts and insights on the delicate subject of religion, spirituality, and life, as I see it. Wherever you happen to be, make yourself comfortable and relaxed so that this may be an enjoyable and meaningful experience for you.

Probably you've asked yourself a few profound questions, such as, Who am I? Why am I here? What is the purpose of life? The answers seem hard to find. Have you noticed how the more you know about a certain subject, the more you realize how much more there is to discover? Or to put it another way, the more you know, the more you become aware of what you don't know? It's a paradox, and life is full of paradoxes, and until we understand that, life seems very confusing.

I'm making a complicated point, and that is, "the paradox of Truth:"

1) There is no absolute truth, and

2) There is.

In the same way,

A) We create our own destiny, and

B) Life presents our destiny. It's not an either/or situation, but rather a this *and* that situation.

What I'm saying is that everything is a matter of understanding. When I was three years old, I believed that Santa Claus was *real*. When I was six, my truth changed, for I had discovered the illusion, but for the three-year-old, at this time, their truth is that Santa exists!

Life is a series of trial-and-error experiments. What seems true for us today is supplanted by a greater truth as we become more and more aware.

The only real truth that we know for sure is that there is a Highly Intelligent understanding, an all-knowing, loving Power or Force that creates. It is the *Creator* that I choose to call the Spiritual Power. It has many Holy names depending on one's religious background— The Higher Power, The Presence, The Buddha Nature, Nature, Jesus, Allah, Brahma, Jehovah, God, and on and on.

Use the name that *you* feel comfortable with and know That is who I am referring to for you, when I talk of the Universal Power. It is the All-prevailing Spirit. It has always been, is now, and will always be, from eternity to eternity. There never was anything else.

The Bible tells us we are made in That Spiritual Image, just a little lower than the Angels. This means that we are made of this creative Essence, this Spiritual Nature. We are part of it. We are like what the wave is to the ocean. We are not the entire ocean, but one hundred percent of us is of the ocean, and the ocean is one hundred percent of us. Here is another paradox: we are of the same Holy Essence, and although Its entirety is greater than us, yet there is no separation. It is because we are not separate that we are truly brothers and sisters in the "Spirit." The same Essence that keeps your heart beating, keeps my heart beating, yet we are unique. Just as there are no two fingerprints alike, there is nobody in the world exactly the same as you.

Whatever your religion, realize that it is just a stepping stone. There are truths in all religions, and these truths are meant to bring us to the realization that the Spiritual Essence is what *we are*.

When we reach this level of understanding, we seek mainly the *truth* from within ourselves, for that is where it is untampered by man's good intentions and conflicting opinions. Let's heed our own hunches, and let our own conscience become our guide.

We are all necessary, individual cogs in the wheel of life, and we have a destiny to fulfill. We are both insignificant and *all* important at the same time. We are here by design of the great Architect of the Universe, the Universal Power.

We have different personalities, and we are free to make mistakes and to learn from the consequences. It's the law of cause and effect. When we make the right choices, we have heavenly results. The wrong ones give us hellish results. I believe that heaven or hell is not some place in the sky after we're dead, but right here, right now, in exact proportion to our thinking and subsequent actions. As you think in your heart, so you behave. Love begets love. Hate begets hate.

Know that you are a *perfect* child of the Essence that IS. Don't just hear what I am saying with your ears, feel what I am saying in your heart. You are one hundred percent part of Perfection. The real you is a Perfect, loving, creative, beautiful you.

You may say that is blasphemy, that you've been taught you are a sinner. Exactly. That's what you've been taught, and that's what you've believed and felt guilty about. Certainly we all sin (make mistakes), and we can constructively learn from them, but for me, it is more important to show my appreciation of the Spiritual Creator for creating me, and to live up to the highest potential that is inherent within me, than to dwell on my mistakes.

I think that we hurt ourselves by making unkind choices, but I do not believe that we can hurt the Universal Power, which knows that as the fog of misunderstanding clears, our perfection begins to show through; as we grow and get our bloated ego out of the way, our True self shines through.

Ego is one of the biggest errors we need to overcome, for it blinds us from the truth. The truth is that we are all *One*, so how can I be greater or lesser than you? I may be different from you in my actions or knowledge, but I am of the same perfect essence, neither higher nor lower than you.

The main confusion that occurs is because each of us is like two people. One is the Spiritual Self, the other the ego or personality self. Sometimes the belief is that as we become more educated and are able to cope egotistically, we start thinking how great we are. Some people flaunt this attitude by arguing to prove that they are always right.

Such conceit and ego seems to close off any need for our Spiritual Power, but we might be humbled when we realize we're comprised of seventy percent water. That's rather insignificant! When we consider our Spiritual-self with unlimited potential, surely a wise course to follow is to let our Spiritual Power direct us.

Our Spiritual-self functions from a fourth dimensional, spiritual plane of understanding and is complete perfection and all-knowing. Our ego or worldly personality self is somewhat less than that, because it has learned the ways of the world through its experiences in this world. We have learned much good, but also life in general may have taught us greed, dishonesty, and even errors from well-intending, but misinformed people.

On this third dimension, we deal with feelings, thoughts, education, experiments and experiences, actions and reactions, hurts and joys, negative and positive, health and sickness, and various polarities, on and on.

On the Spiritual Fourth Dimensional Plane, *all* is known, the oneness of unity, beauty, and love. There is no conflict, no polarity, jealousy, or suffering. The Spiritual Power knows its Majesty, and as we are It, at a deep level, we do too.

With this knowledge of how beautiful it will be after this lifetime, don't jump to the conclusion that you've had enough here, thinking that suicide will solve the problem, *it won't!* There is some mechanism that demands we finish out our experiences here on the third dimensional level before entering the fourth dimension.

Built within each of us *is* the fourth dimension, a conscience that helps guide our paths, and when we heed Its call, It steers us in the direction of self-discovery. As we tune into our inner guidance system and learn to depend upon it, we find ourselves tuning in more and more to our fourth dimensional selves.

The great teachers knew this secret very well and informed us that greater things than they, can we do, but first we have to trust and tune in and keep tuning in until the static has disappeared, so that we hear and *know*.

There may be many phases to develop this experience. Some of us have been Atheists. Others, not being able to believe religions taught to them, have become Agnostics. Still others hang onto beliefs because of the fear of hell in the afterlife.

Personally, I have no fear of hell in the afterlife and believe that the only hell we may experience is the hell we create here and now through incorrect instruction, thinking, or behavior.

Begin just exactly where you are in your understanding and develop Faith. Faith is a belief and trust in something unseen that you sense or feel to be true. The Bible says, "Have the faith of a grain of mustard seed." What does this mean? To me it means that small as a mustard seed is, it knows that it will be mustard and not cabbage, lettuce, or potatoes. Inherent in the seed is its ultimate destiny. Everything that it requires to grow is within the seed. Inherent in us is our Spiritual Nature, waiting to be discovered.

As we desire these answers and seek them, so too does our Spiritual Essence desire our knowing, and seeks us. We start from exactly where we are in our thinking, and our desire leads us to have faith. As we practice this Faith in our daily lives, still seeking, this faith grows to become a Knowing, and when we know that we know, *we know!*

So what are the benefits of all of this knowledge? Perhaps the first benefit is not to fear death, but to accept it with joy, in view of the new understanding. Second, we discover there is a way right here and now to tap into the fourth dimensional plane and bring its solutions, health, and beauty into our lives on this third dimensional plane at this time. "To be in this world, but not of it."

How is this achieved? By the blessings of the Spiritual Power. When we are ready, feelings well up within us. Just as at puberty we learned naturally of the sexual feelings, so too does Nature provide us with feelings or experiences that cause us to search out the meanings of life. We are led to these discoveries slowly at first by the injunction, "Seek first your Spiritual Essence, and all else, (ALL, ALL,

ALL else) will be added unto you." These are no idle words. We need to heed them.

With this awareness, we see things clearly, and demonstrate in our being (with ease), the few principles that turn us around from being prideful, resentful, and hateful. There is no longer a need to prove yourself. By just "being," (letting go and letting our Spiritual Essence surface), we become who we really are. We come to discover the paradox that, "In the giving of your love is the receiving of it," and that "You can never give too much love, for its supply is unlimited."

Again, please pause and contemplate.

Expanded Religion

A speaker, talking about religion and spiritual teachings was asked, "I am so confused, I've visited a half-dozen different religious meetings, and each one claims theirs to the be right one, and theirs alone. How can I tell which is correct?" I was appalled by his reply, "Mine is!"

What is the purpose of religion, and how did it come about? What are some of the results? While wrestling with the paradoxes of life, what seemed to be emerging for me was the need for our personality to blend and harmonize with our spiritual consciousness, to outgrow the differences and discover our Unity, while maintaining our individuality.

It seems that religion, which teaches truths, is just a "first step" in self-discovery, and can actually be the very shackle to keep us locked into the past experiences, allegories, rituals, and dogmas. I see its purpose as being a guide map to discovering "Inner Peace," contentment, love, and understanding, or, as some call It, God, or Peace.

Religion probably came about through consciousness, and as humans felt an inner need, rules and regulations were established. Often fears were developed to fill this need. People were very superstitious and tended to follow dogmas, as sheep. Even today some people feel that it is okay to kill "in the name of God," and unholy wars are still prevalent. What illusion or deception could possibly hoodwink us into believing that we should kill in the name of, or for the benefit of, God? Surely killing Its very creation must be contrary to Its plan.

My aim is to bridge the gap of confusion and frustration that separates and distracts us from the goal of each of us in our own way or belief, to attain our highest principles.

Assuming that God is a God of Love, would It choose only a certain religion for heaven, and for all others (even those who have not even heard of the religion) to be damned eternally? I think that God would be fairer than that.

There have been many outstanding and holy men and women, and the followers of each belief feel very strongly about them. If we study Eastern religions, the beliefs are that the God Force is everywhere in every thing—the trees, rivers, and people. It is easy then to understand why there were many Gods that appear in the form of Rain Gods and Gods of Fire.

In Judaism, Abraham conceived of only one God, all others being sacrilegious. Thus it was when Christianity proclaimed Jesus to be the God child, Jews could not (because of their beliefs) accept him—rather they are still waiting for the Messiah to appear, as are Christians waiting for the return of Christ. I wonder if the Messiah or Christ were to arrive on the scene, if anyone would recognize Him?

By what signs or understanding could we recognize the coming of the Messiah or the return of Christ? Just perhaps the Christ's or Messiah's arrival is the Essence of what all religions purport to teach: Love, discovered in our own hearts, revealing the Messiah or Christ Spirit though us as the expression of Love.

We house that Universal Spirit. As and when we realize it, we are It, each one of us. When we learn this, there is no longer need for the Ten Commandments, for with this Love, we'd already be incorporating them. Unconditional love from within, first for ourselves, then for our neighbors, starts with me, but does not end with me.

Now the time has come that we emerge from our cocoons and soar, to wake up and find our individual pathways home, and to understand that we are each a child of the Universal Spirit, or, to put it a little differently, an individual cell—with a personalized function necessary for the whole, in the body of "Life."

The Eternal, in Its wisdom, created us to be unique, similar perhaps, but *unique*. How boring life might have been otherwise. In Its wisdom also was the precious gift of freedom to express this uniqueness, or to put it another way, "Freedom of Choice." Freedom of choice is a remarkable thing, and as we mature, we choose it with responsibility and appreciation of our ability to take charge of our lives. I guess the argument can be made that anyone who seeks to dominate our freedom is actually working counter to that Universal Power's gift, so that it's up to us as an individual, and collectively, to maintain the courage of pursuing our individual uniqueness, lovingly. We no longer need to be victims.

It has been said that, "The one thing we can be certain of is change." Although we may not always want it, it seems to be part of evolution. Many people, comfortable where they are, feel very threatened by changes and put their finger in the dike, trying to hold back the waters. Others though, have welcomed the new experiences with all their challenges. How do you feel and respond to change? Are you in favor of individual choices, or opposed? Can we agree to differ?

Is it possible that the spokes of all religions lead to a *central hub* of Spiritual Power? Can we live and let live, loving *all* of the Spiritual Nature's children, colors, creeds, and languages? Indeed, the challenge is ours, and it's an exciting new opportunity awaiting us. The computer age has already brought us to the place where education alone is inadequate. We no sooner learn something, than it becomes obsolete. It's hard to keep up with all of the incoming knowledge. Just as we are leaving earth to discover space and interplanetary challenges, so the time has come for us to expand our minds and leave the limitations of our thinking to our consciousness, to tune into the higher frequencies of wisdom, through understanding and intuition. Knowledge may no longer be the answer, unless used to express our Inner Wisdom or guidance.

Religion points the way; some grasp its message, others miss it or get frustrated. Some get caught up on a religious ego trip of superiority. Many get hypnotized to keep coming back for more of the same, afraid or unwilling to expand. Seek first the Spiritual Power, and all else will be added unto you. But where to seek this Spirituality? We seem to search everywhere, except within for self-discovery, or if you prefer, for revelation. We need to look within. How might we best seek this Inner-Self? What we've been doing is trying to reach the spiritual frequency from a physical frequency. It's like trying to get an FM program on an AM frequency. It doesn't often happen.

When we are awake, we are said to be conscious, when asleep, unconscious. Science tells us of the different states of consciousness: Alpha, Beta, Delta, and Theta. And we're discovering how to attain these different states of consciousness at will, with great benefit to our physical and mental well-being, as in Biofeedback.

The paradox of, "Be in the world, but not of it," to me, means to function on an earthly plane, while following the guidance of our Spiritual Consciousness, and streamlining and concentrating our actions along that pathway."

As a matter of interest, my beliefs are not the same now as they were fifteen years ago, and I hope in the years to come to have insights that may work for me even better in the future. Meanwhile, I do the best I can with what I have, patiently growing one step at a time, *enjoying the journey* in as much harmony and love as I can muster through meditation, contemplation, and Being the Love.

We need to know that the Power, Essence, Spirit, Nature, Energy, God, Universal Power is Unconditional Love or Peace, and that we are that Love. To the extent that we recognize this and let it "gush out" through our heart centers, to this extent will we enjoy Utopia in our own lives and hasten its approach for others right here on Planet Earth.

Some tools for these expressions are: Instead of trying to duplicate someone else, or be what someone else expects us to be, we need to be who we are. We need to be our highest self, appreciate the freedom we've discovered, and allow others their space, also. Know that we are all unfolding at different rates of *time* and that that is okay. Our job is just to BE. For me that includes being true to myself, being happy, healthy, and loving everyone as myself, but not necessarily agreeing with their actions. I express this joy for life, not only during special holidays, but each day, for truly, each day is a Special day. This is a day that the Universe has provided, so let us rejoice in it and appreciate our abundant blessings.

Again, please pause here.

Variety Is the Spice of Life

It has been said that variety is the spice of life. How true that is, and how fortunate we are because we have it. Can you imagine how bland, dull, and boring it would be if everyone's car was painted green? If all houses were identical and their furnishings the same? If there was only one species of tree or flower? If *all* the birds were sparrows, and only codfish in the sea? Imagine the confusion if we all looked the same and dressed alike. I could go on and on with examples.

Variety is not only the spice of life, but a requirement. The Universal Power has blessed us with an abundance of it all: just look at the variety of everything; even identical twins differ, and no two snowflakes that have ever fallen are identical. Can you imagine the *Intelligence* of what It is that can think up and create so many differences? I sit in awe just contemplating it. Yes, the Universal Power is Awesome!

We have all of these marvelous gifts, and yet we balk at them. Instead of savoring the differences, we condemn them for being different, and the one harmonizing similarity we *choose* to ignore.

We tend to ignore completely that the Spiritual Power is in each of us, and that It is everywhere, in everything. There is not a spot where It is not. "I Am That I Am." I AM the sun and the stars, the world and the galaxies, the discovered and the undiscovered. I AM the totality of everything, from the largest to the smallest. The Spiritual Power is not only within us, It is US. We are It, a hundred percent. The purpose of life, as I see it, is to learn and to understand that— to believe it, trust it, and demonstrate it. This is why 2,000 years ago a wonderful teacher was able to demonstrate what man/woman can graduate to be and claim, "Greater things than I, shall ye do." Though in our hearts we may know this to be true, in our heads we just won't believe it. How could this be possible?

With the wonderful gift of freedom of choice, man has made the wrong choices. We've made errors and created egos to be so strong that we deny our Spiritual Essence and insist on proving our own greatness. We cover up our mistakes with so many excuses until we finally believe that our ego knows, and we've come to accept that as a way of life. We need to see this and want to change, to seek Spiritual Wisdom from within and to learn from our mistakes.

What are we out to prove? What is so difficult about letting go and letting our Spiritual Power take over?

We have been taught conformity. I do not say there should be chaos, but what's happened to our originality, our uniqueness, our individuality, and our self-expression? We've been taught that our differences are not to be tolerated, that we need to conform, stifle our common sense and originality, judge others who don't conform, and criticize, complain, and condemn them. This forces them or encourages them to react. That's why society is so fragmented. Judgment and manipulation are robbing us of our freedom. We must stop allowing ourselves to be victims and develop a strong, calm strength of faith and knowing, rather than grovel in a reaction from fear. The truth is that we are more alike than different, yet we need to savor our individual uniqueness and seek the unity in the diversity. If we don't, we'll be left with unsatisfactory and destructive results.

Our Spiritual self is already perfect; we need to align our physical selves to this perfection. For the egotist, it is scary to let the Spiritual Power lead the way, instead of her/his own will. Yet there is nothing to fear. We need to let go of the insecure security blanket (the treadmill of trying to prove our egotistical greatness), and humble ourselves to our Spiritual Nature's greatness, with faith, which in time develops into a Knowing. Know the Truth, and the Truth will set you free, but you have to seek it. How do you seek it?

Start exactly where you are, and open your mind wide to new ideas and possibilities. Our Spiritual Essence lies dormant, eager, yet patiently within each of us, waiting to be discovered when we make the choice to do so, not before!

Develop, on a daily basis, the principles that we know to be true, starting with honesty. Don't steal; be honest with yourself and in your relationships; don't lie to anyone. Be truthful, yet loving; start by loving yourself (the Spirit within). Don't be too harsh with your errors. Forgive yourself and learn not to repeat your mistakes. Forgive others too. This frees you to discern, not judge. Loosen up, and don't be too serious. Life is to be enjoyed. See the humor in things. Be joyful, playful and sometimes serious, but not solemn. Laugh a lot, and look for the good in everything. Hold a genuine respect for yourself and others, and develop understanding in yourself, and it will help you to understand others.

The Universal Power that you seek is within *you*. That is where you will find it. You are It. It is personified in the form of *you*. As you come to know this, you will function more from these higher frequencies in love and understanding, and then you will realize the examples of Moses, Buddha, Jesus, and more recently, Gandhi, are not just their miracles, but our heritage waiting to be believed and claimed by each of us. We are all in different stages of self-discovery, learning to believe that, I too, can do greater things.

Pause and contemplate.

The Miraculous Computer

Approximately in the year 1900, the horseless carriage replaced the horse and buggy. Soon came the sound of wireless and the appearance of great flying birds called airplanes. In those days you may have been locked up as being insane had you talked about such things as flying to and landing on the moon. Nevertheless, new and unimagined things like TV came into use, bringing at the press of a button people, sounds, and scenery from around the world, and, even more astounding, from outer space. In the short span from 1900 to date, the impossibility of flight to the moon, Venus, Mars and beyond, has become a reality.

To build craft to accomplish such feats, has entailed the use of computers to calculate, manufacture, and operate these marvels of ingenious transportation, and constant computer improvements have been necessary. However, there is already in existence a computer that has been fed perfect answers for everything, yet is so light and compact that a child can carry and operate it. The computer that I'm referring to is our brain. When we tune into our Universal Power, all information is available as in a computer that has been fed perfect answers.

What makes the brain function is an electric force, without which the fantastic brain, or even the incredible heart, is rendered useless. It is this Universal Power or Spiritual Nature, inherent in us all, that feeds the brain the intuitive creative thoughts that materialize through our action. With this awareness, the benefit of higher intuitive thoughts become more obvious, but the method of attaining them may not be as obvious, so you might ask, how? A few pointers may be:

1) Give up pride, resentment, hatred, bigotry, and violence, to improve our receptivity.

2) Dare to live by your heart's instinct or inner voice, allowing it to bring out the best in you, to live each day in the pattern you choose to adopt.

3) I give thanks that, like you, I am a miraculous computer, and especially for the awareness of its driving energy, the Universal Power.

Understanding Religious Differences

I was fortunate to attend the Centennial Meeting of the World Parliament of Religions in Chicago in August/September 1993. At that meeting, many spiritual leaders searched for ways to bridge the gap of misunderstanding among the diversified religions, while taking a non-judgmental, broad-minded approach.

Just as a specific background and language work well to communicate within a particular country, so too do different religions fit the needs of a varied and searching people. It's not that one religion is better than another, but rather that each one is different. The intent of most of them is to lead to Love, Tolerance, Understanding of what God is, our relationship to that Universal Power, and how best this understanding can benefit the whole of humanity!

The one thing that all religions point to is that there is a Supernatural, All-Intelligent, Creative *something* that has created, and is creating, everything. Within each of us lies that Spiritual Power awaiting our discovery, and we need to realize that. Instead of struggling to get love or trying to be good, we need to know we already are Spiritually *perfect*. When we learn this, we desire to come from this place of love effortlessly, and with incredible results.

Without the ego act, we become confident and strong enough to express the love in our hearts without fear of criticism or that people may take advantage of us.

When they know the truth for themselves, they will no longer criticize. Usually people criticize others because they are afraid or unwilling to examine themselves. We have *nothing* to fear. We are co-creators with the Spiritual Essence. Any mistakes we have made because of our unawareness at the time, is a learning opportunity to forgive ourselves immediately and to know we are forgiven only when we forgive ourselves. It doesn't matter about what happened yesterday. Today is a brand new day. It is what we do from now on that counts. And, oh, yes, we will make more mistakes, for life is a continual learning process. We gradually make less of them as we learn to be tolerant of ourselves and others. Then we become more relaxed and function better as a result of it. Remember how uptight and inefficient we were when we were learning to drive a car, and how easy it became when we improved? Life is like this, too. We need to stop paddling against the stream, to go with the flow and grow. Be gentle with yourself. You are precious.

Contemplate.

All in a Lifetime

What came first, the chicken or the egg? To be interesting, we need to be interested. I was talking with a bright and happy "young" man of 96 years and his younger brother of 94. What a privilege, and yet how incredible that I could be talking with people who were born before the electric light bulb was discovered, who witnessed the automobile become a reality. They were alive even before radio was discovered, and yet during their lifetimes they are now witnessing a Magic Box called TV in their living room. Now, not only are people being propelled to visit the moon and return, but they are building cities in space, all in one lifetime. Things have changed drastically, yet paradoxically, haven't they? After all, electricity has been here forever, but it wasn't discovered until recently.

With accumulated knowledge, computers, and other miracles of the modern age, scientists have discovered quantum physics and proved the existence of invisible energy in the form of atoms, neutrons, and electrons. And for the first time, they are getting in step with instead of opposing religion and the mystics who have known of this invisible energy throughout the ages. This incredible energy that keeps the heart of the 96/94-year-olds beating is the same Energy Force or power that beats in the heart of a baby, while still in its mother's womb.

It is the one prevailing force that we have in common, the one element which we share whether we are a murderer, crook, or a holy person. This element in nature, the Life Force, is to be found in everything, the air we breathe, flowers, animals, birds, and fish. Spiritual Nature is the constant, changeless energy that is changing everything. It patiently watches humankind as it makes its painful, turbulent way through wars and other self-destructing holocausts, on its journey to discover that we are all part of the same Nature, that we have just been fighting ourselves, when we could be loving ourselves and one another.

As we're each a unique cell in the body of life, there is no separation, and life goes on and on from one plateau of experience to the next on an ever upward, spiraling journey of understanding, wisdom, and peace.

Please contemplate.

Beginning to Know

Life is made up of polarities/paradoxes:

Positives and Negatives . . . Knowing and Fear.

In our search for understanding, we frequently turn inward for self-discovery. Often, since we've learned to be "Positive," we put on an outside front that all is okay, while on the inside, we tear ourselves apart, wanting to be what we're pretending to be! It's not that we're wanting to be hypocritical, but rather we're taught that if you act the part, you become it. To a limited extent, this is true.

The underlying problem the world has is *fear*. From it stems feelings of inadequacy, frustration, anger, violence, resentment, and hatred, also the need for chemical crutches, such as drugs and alcohol.

We live in a world of *fear*. Everything is based on it—armies, police forces, industry, and employees all contribute to increase this catastrophe!

The Bible admonishes us to be in this world, but not of it, meaning that we live and function on Planet Earth, but, rather than follow the group consciousness or thinking, we need to come from our Spiritual Knowing. I've spent half my lifetime trying to come from this knowing place, but although I've felt *it* to be within my grasp, I hadn't mastered it. What was I doing wrong? Let's start with, what was I doing? Perhaps you've had similar experiences.

Having travelled through formal religions and comparative religions, I've come to accept that there is one Universal Power, an indescribably intelligent Energy Force, that has always been, is, and always will be. We are all children of that Spiritual Nature. There is nothing else existing but It, in form and formlessness. Therefore, we are of this Supreme Energy Force, co-creators, if you will. We are constantly creating, knowingly or not, planned or haphazard. Our manifestations stem from our thinking. Our thinking has been learned from our environment (group consciousness), which with few exceptions, is negative. World thinking concentrates on *fear*. How can we change this?

With our freedom of choice and much seeking, we can eventually choose to follow our Universal Power while still here on earth. The big question is how to attain this. As we believe that our individual Messiah is within, the doors to nature's laws open and we accept our Spiritual inheritance with all of its miraculous opportunities, and they become a normal function. We need to *trust*.

My efforts to do that were exactly that: my efforts. I thought, pondered, begged, pleaded, prayed, searched, questioned, studied, talked, listened, hoped, knew (intellectually), and meditated to discover the secret, so near and yet so far off. Seek first the Spiritual Power, and all else will be added unto you; ALL, ALL, ALL else. Can you conceive of what that means? Talk about a pearl of great price! Where is the key? I think I have grasped it. Time will show if I have.

If, as earlier stated, we come from *fear*-oriented thinking, our search, although enlightening, keeps returning us to feelings of insecurity or unworthiness: Although I keep trying, still I think I am failing. I can't. I'm not good enough. I'm only human. I want to do God's will only, but what is it? How do I know? Doubts, doubts, doubts. More questions, more insecurity, still no satisfactory answers. Why? More learning, more studies, constant frustration, and more guilt because of it. After all, by now I *should* know better! Perhaps, just perhaps, I'm working too hard trying to do it from here, and it can't be done from here.

Our thinking is *fear*-oriented, fear of again failing in the very discovery that we seek. Therefore, the next attempt has to be different. We've often heard the saying, "Let go and go with the flow." Now we need to bring this idea to life. Stop efforting and desperately searching with an earthly method on an earthly plane, and seek the kingdom of a Higher Consciousness *in* a Higher Consciousness, effortlessly.

Let go of our trying to do it and Let our Spiritual Nature perform. How to do this effortlessly? First by becoming appreciative of the beauty of nature that surrounds us everywhere in myriad forms. Read some inspirational writings: the Bible, affirmations, poetry. Ponder on them for awhile. Then, while in this frame of mind, meditate, and in this calm, allow your mind to go blank and experience the Everything/Nothingness from which ALL is created. The Spiritual plane of consciousness does not act on our earthly memories and mistakes of the past on which to build the unknown future, but offers us the moment-to-moment experience of the Now for us to live in and build upon. We can then transform this higher intelligent knowing onto the earthly plane, literally performing miracles, healings, and manifestations. So, literally let go and trust your Universal Power. Perhaps now is the time to rest and not get so caught up in studies and reading, but rather in contemplating, giving the mind time to assimilate the wisdom you're seeking.

Again, please contemplate.

CHAPTER FIFTEEN

Beliefs and Insights

What I Believe (in a nutshell)

WHAT I BELIEVE is that there is a Universal Power, and that It is an intangible energy that Is. It is a creative intelligence that abounds yet, like air, cannot be seen. However, the effects are everywhere. There is no place that It does not exist, for It is all there is. Everything is part of It, and It is a part of everything and everybody, everything that is, including the void, everything.

Many mystics have been aware of this power and have learned to demonstrate it in their lives. Their experiences are an external reminder of the power/essence that we all are/have, and that we too can demonstrate it.

The question then is, if we are this Power, why aren't we demonstrating it? The answer is that we are, that we express and create, but we can only demonstrate as we understand It. Because of Its nature, It has to create, and as people we are one of the vehicles chosen to express or channel this creation. We have been given the freedom of choice to produce with It whatever we will. We have demonstrated this ability in tangible ways and have created miracles in the form of things. We have harnessed electricity. Our discovery of air waves, creation of radio, aircraft, spacecrafts and skyscrapers are all miracles of our co-creative minds.

We are in the process of discovering that our conscious choices are the *molds* that the Energy flows into and then becomes materialized.

We have to reeducate our minds into believing and accepting who we are, as it is difficult for us to accept our vastness. Somehow we have to conceive of the inconceivable miracle. We are the Miracle of Life, empowered to direct the Energy flow for the benefit of humanity. We are complete and whole. Nothing needs to be added or taken away. I, my whole body, is Peace Pilgrim II. My right hand is not my whole body; it is not my mind or my chest, but one hundred percent of my hand is part of me. Similarly, I am not the Universal Power in Its entirety, but one hundred percent of me is of that Spiritual Nature, one hundred percent. It is important to *know* this, believe it, and live according to it. The Creative Force requires that we express and create, give and receive.

Paraphrasing The Lord's Prayer

Our Spiritual Essence that is within us,
Love is Thy name.
Illuminate our wisdom, that we may recognize It,
For your kingdom Is the heaven within us.
We thankfully live *this* day.
Let us give others their viewpoints, while respecting our own.
As we let go of our egos, *encourage* our true selves to shine.
For in me lies your kingdom, power, and glory,
Dormant, until my discovery of It.
Regardless of Its future form or formlessness, It is forever.
For I AM That I AM. I AM.

In Depth Version of The Lord's Prayer

Infinite Power, we are in awe of You.
Open up our receptivity to Your energy flow,
That we may claim our abundance.
Guide our understanding so that we no longer judge others,
So that even the desire to forgive them does not need to apply,
And let us be equally lenient with *ourselves.*
Strengthen the knowing of our true Nature,
So that it dominates our ego,
Enabling us to recognize that
We are personified forms of the One Essence.
Amen.

O Great Consciousness

O Great Consciousness of the Universe,
We are in Awe of You.
Help us to "tune-in" to your consciousness,
That we may live by that guidance here on Planet Earth.
Give us this day our daily needs/requirements,
And alert us not to stay/stray into our egos,
But strengthen us to overcome pride.
Encourage the forgiveness of ourselves and others,
That we may live Understanding Lives,
Emulating Your Awesome Love.
For Love is of your kingdom and Power.
YOU ARE THE ALL.

Unifying for Peace

Considering the millions of churches, temples, and other houses of worship that exist, we should be asking why are there still wars and so much turmoil in our lives. In order to solve a problem, it has to be defined.

We have seen in the chapterette, "Variety is the Spice of Life," how mundane life would be if there wasn't diversity. I think such limitations would be hard to accept. In Its wisdom, brilliance, and magnificence, our Universal Power has given us the blessings of abundant diversity, and for too long we have fought for exclusivity, rather than seeking the joys of inclusiveness. When will we celebrate the wonder of our differences as we do the variety of foods that diverse cultures offer us?

It's as if we have felt that Unity means being a carbon copy of one another, but just the contrary is true. Unity offers us the strength to follow our own chosen religion or belief system, while respecting, appreciating, and encouraging others with their freedom of choice, to follow their own chosen pathway.

I believe that individual religions are the diversified spokes joining the Holy hub, and that it is for us to add the rim of harmony to join the spokes, so we may together create a wheel of life to function for the glory of the Creator and for the benefit of human-kind.

Let us rejoice in the abundance and truly appreciate the unity of our diversity, by reaching out to the top ranking religious leaders to send out to all the houses of worship a directive to influence their hundreds and thousands of congregations that:

We cannot allow more religious killings, or any other killing. Without Peace, everything is threatened—our families, our homes, our jobs, our possessions, and indeed, our lives.

Our Top Priority has to become Peace, and Peace requires a massive, mature education of self-examination, and an earnest desire to improve our individual Peace efforts. Our behavior and actions influence others either in constructive or destructive ways.

Unconditional love thrives on awareness, beauty, and soul-searching. Therefore, let us not merely talk God, but by example express unconditional love. We have to walk the talk! So perhaps if the congregations are "ordered" by top religious leaders everywhere that *any* killing will not be tolerated, we'll begin to see glimpses of cooperation.

The Golden Rule

(a guide to living as seen from different religious viewpoints)

Christianity Therefore all things whatsoever ye would that men should do to you, do ye even so to them.

Judaism And thou shalt love thy neighbor as thyself.

Hinduism Good people proceed while considering what is best for others is best for themselves.

Bahá'í Ascribe not to any soul that which thou wouldst not have ascribed to thee. And say not that which thou doest not. This is my command unto thee, do thou observe it.

Zoroastrianism Whatever is disagreeable to yourself, do not do unto others.

Buddhism Hurt not others with that which pains yourself.

Islam No one of you is a believer until he loves for his brother what he loves for himself.

Confucianism What you do not want done to yourself, do not do unto others.

The different Gods/Religions that we worship seem to be saying the same thing, differently. It's time to move beyond the bickering of our religious differences and to unite under the Rainbow of the Universal Power that encompasses the truths of all religions. Let us grasp Its essence now.

Adapted from Corinthians

Though I speak with authority, but do not have love in my heart, I speak empty words, and though I have much knowledge and all faith, yet do not have love, it is of little value.

Though I'm generous with money, and keep busy doing things and working, and still do not have love, it's really been a waste of time.

Love suffers long and is kind; it does not envy anything or anybody.

Love is giving, Love knows no pride but knows to live the Golden Rule—it prefers to give rather than to receive. Realizing the futility of strife, it is not easily provoked.

It does not entertain evil thoughts about anything or anybody. It is not happy in injustice, but enjoys the truth.

Love accepts life as it comes, believing that the Universe is unfolding as it should, hoping for the best, yet enduring all things. Love is the key to Life.

Insights

For the purposes of sharing insights, let us talk about the mineral, plant, animal, and human kingdoms, as they seem to be the main ones exposed to us at present on this planet, and let us always remember that it's the Spiritual kingdom that creates, encompasses, includes, guides, rules, and governs All.

The Mineral Kingdom. As part of our needs on this planet, the Universal Power has given us the minerals to observe Its majestic beauty in the forms of mountains for our use in building materials and in other precious minerals for creating jewels.

Mineral is the Universal Power created by Itself as stone, oil, or whatever. It has life and is comprised of movement, such as atoms, electrons, and maybe intelligences that at this time we know nothing about.

The Plant and Vegetable Kingdom. All plants and vegetables have life. They grow, and the light of the sun helps them. Like us, they have feelings, respond to *Love*, music, and other stimuli, yet unlike the minerals, they require oxygen and water.

The plant life has also been given to us for our sustenance: trees for the building of homes and furniture, flowers for beauty to feast our eyes and hearts on so we may feel the spirit that grows them, and plants for medical purposes; and, through all of these subtleties, to come to know It, our Universal Power.

The Animal Kingdom. This kingdom, including the fish and fowl, is the one most visible to us, and much of our learning seems to have stemmed from and to be coming from it. This animal kingdom is again a gift to us from our Spiritual Nature, as is everything else. It is also here for our pleasure, learning, beauty, and understanding.

Animals have behavioral patterns serving different needs. They mainly kill only for food and react to danger by either fight or flight. There are kingdoms within kingdoms. For example, the ants have their own world, interests, leaders, and specific business of what they're doing. Birds migrate (just what navigates them?!). Fish spawn at certain places each year, and they know how to get there! The wonders, understanding, and intelligence of this kingdom are not to be underestimated, and today's studies are coming up with incredible findings.

The Human Kingdom. It's as though, in our lifetime, we experience three different stages:

1) The Undeveloped Human Kingdom
2) The Growing Human Kingdom
3) The Understanding or Spiritual Kingdom

This subject is so vast that even if I had the full understanding of it, my brief version of it would have to encompass volumes. I'll do my best to condense the highlights as I understand them.

For reasons, whatever they may be, we've been sent to this planet, maybe on a mission or a spiritual lab investigation. I'm convinced we are part of the Great Universal Spirit, that we were once fully of that kingdom and that when we have completed our stay on this planet, we return to it or go forward to a higher plateau. At this time I do not choose to discuss the hereafter, but to confine myself mainly with our present habitat, for the purpose of explanation, to show where we came from. We came from a Holy place!

We entered into a world of Fear. The game plan, as I understand it, is to attain the Holy place here for ourselves, then to share it with others, so that we may create Heaven on earth, where the lion and the lamb are together, blissfully.

When we enter the world, we are probably pure and aware of our Spiritual Essence, except for a few preconceived circumstances that exist to give us our uniqueness. This individuality is our contribution to create or destroy this planet, or maybe for the discovery of other planets. Therefore, our personal creation here is to be tempered by the genes inherent in our DNA, the background of our parents and their parents, going perhaps all the way back.

For our purposes, let's start with conception, the very nature of it being extremely competitive, so that of the millions of sperm, only one or a few succeed in fertilizing the female egg. Thus, though we don't seem to want to believe it, we are actually born winners. To digress for a moment, though we are winners, we don't seem to allow ourselves to believe it. The fact is that we house the Spiritual Essence. It's what we *are*, and we need to appreciate it.

The God spirit is already *here*—there is nothing to search "out there" for. It's already encompassed, given to us free, a gift through no earnings of our own, just as everything else has been given to us free to use or abuse, condemn and ignore, or marvel and appreciate. In addition, we have the most wonderful of gifts, the Freedom of Choice.

We can choose Illumination or fight It, but we get to experience the consequences. However, we've been shown the way; the guidepost is clear. Seek first the Universal Power, and all else will be added unto you.

Going back to conception, at the time of conception, the DNA and genes form part of our life, and for perhaps the briefest moment of conception, our parents were in bliss, at peace, united in Love with one another and with the Spiritual Power that formed them and you. But after that moment, they were again their human selves, whatever their state of living was. If it was loving, kind, and blissful, it had an affect on you. If it was disrespectful, belligerent, yelling, screaming, etc., that too had an affect. And if it included drinking, smoking, drugs, or disease, it may have had a drastic affect of whether you were indeed to be born on this material plane, or born deformed, physically defective, or mentally deranged. I do not pretend to know the reasons for all of this, but the Universal Spirit sees, knows, and creates, and It knows the big picture. I trust explicitly that in this big picture, the Universe is unfolding as it should, and I believe that. Our lives are predestined *and* we have a choice as to how we fulfill this destiny.

The Undeveloped Human Kingdom. In the beginning of our lives, I do not feel that we have too much choice, as we come into the undeveloped human kingdom, where we're at the mercy of circumstances and learning influences from different personal experiences, to discover our world and how we're to function in it. We discover our ego, and it drives us on. Sometimes we get caught up in the wheel of life until it becomes too much and we scream to come off. There's lots of confusing, good-intending help out there, and we grasp at straws and reach out to the next step.

The Growing Human Kingdom. Here, I believe the very things that did not work on the lower plane of understanding (the undeveloped human kingdom), are the rules that work to draw us from the undeveloped human kingdom towards our final evolutionary destiny, with the Universal Power.

In our undeveloped human kingdom, we had feelings of power and conquest over others. We reacted to others or we acted on impulse and used violence to secure our desires. It was necessary to recognize those feelings and transmute them into constructive action.

Jesus speaks of loving your neighbor *as* yourself, suggesting that we see the Spiritual Power in ourselves and in others too, *and to do unto others*. Much of His teachings are unconditional love, compassion, tolerance, understanding, wisdom, patience, and looking for the beauty in the *sinners,* to help them recognize it. He taught by *demonstration,* expressing the Spiritual Power and being constantly in harmony and in touch with It.

Not through my ability, but through the understanding of the Universal Power am I willing to be my highest self, to explore whatever it takes to help myself and others evolve too.

The Understanding, Spiritual Kingdom. This is the Ultimate place on Earth, with spiritual understanding a constant. Guidelines for growing into this awareness, as I see it, are: pondering on nature, reading inspirational books to get the gist of what they're saying, meditation, lectures and classes, but mainly living in *today,* expressing the *Love* that is in your heart, in all that you think, say and do, and to be in awe of the Spiritual Power's creation with constant appreciation of It. Especially appreciate, believe, and accept that we are Co-creators with It. Know, don't doubt, that we house that Spiritual Power, that Rainbow of Spirit, the *unlimited* potential in its fullness and entirety, as much as we can comprehend. Constantly, painfully, slowly, grasping more, we relax into the knowingness, giving up the struggle of fighting to know, but giving in to Its grace to show us, in Its time, what we are to comprehend *today.*

Ours is to be the lighthouse through which the Universal Power illuminates us and the world. Love knows no boundaries. It is highly contagious and, as our Source, It is unlimited. Know your Spiritual Power and get on with your life. Don't spend your life finding It. It *is* your life, to be fully lived, this moment, *now* and each moment, as

the expression of your uniqueness and appreciation for the bounty
It has given to you.
Contemplate.

On a Spiritual Note

The teacher, Jesus, in I is wisdom realized that of himself, he was
nothing, but that the Essence within, does the work. His understanding of the higher energies were expressed in his unconditional love
of all peoples of the world. Whereas he loved the people, realizing
their holiness, he did not condone their actions or behavior. He, in
his brilliance, was able to discern the person from the action *without*
judgment. So great was his understanding and love, that to this day,
his teachings are still taught, though much of his wisdom is misun-
derstood and misinterpreted.

He has given us clues to follow, such as, "I and the Father are
One," "Greater things than I shall you do," and "I am the way." But
so awesome are these statements that we refuse to take them at face
value for fear of having to accept the responsibility of *truth*.

I see "the way" to be an understanding that the Universal Power
is in all of us waiting to be recognized, and invited by us to flow
through us as unconditional love to the world, not just to a select few.
We need to let go of our hearts of stone, to open up our hearts of
Love.

If the Spiritual Power loves everyone, all of Its children, doesn't
it behoove us to do the same? How dare any of us do otherwise. The
denial of this is reflected in our wars and turmoil. Clearly we have
been spoken to. To love ourselves as children of our Spiritual
Essence, and to know that whereas our behavior may need to be
improved, still our Essence is perfect. We need to love our neighbors
as ourselves, for they too are of this Holy Essence. If and when they
understand this, their behavior too will change to conform to their
true beauty. But they do not understand, and fear has kept, and *is*
keeping them from trying. We need to trust and appreciate the
magnificence of the Universal Power in all of Its creation, and all of

Its diversity, with Its brilliance and wondrous creation. Still we remain in ignorance and unawareness, and fight one another with bigotry, prejudice, judgment, anger, hatred, and wars. When will we *celebrate* the wonder of our differences and diversified cultures? Truly unconditional love is the answer to all of our problems, and *nothing* is more important than to learn to apply this Love.

It is time for all religions to remember that condemning is a judgment and that we are admonished not to judge, lest we be judged. Nature has it that our backgrounds, cultures, upbringing, understanding, languages, ideas, and ideals are all different. We are all on the evolutionary path of self-discovery, each in our own way, and each in our own time. We cannot unfold the rose, but when the heart is ready, it will unfold on its own accord.

Therefore, let us truly embrace one another with acceptance, as the one big family that we are, and learn to love one another.

The time to do this is now! The way to change is through unconditional love. The counters are loaded with self-help books, and there are groups of people everywhere learning these changes. There are no longer excuses for ignorance or apathy. Peace and love begin with me. Each one of us needs to share in this privilege and responsibility, NOW!

Peace on earth and good will towards all men and women can no longer be an annual slogan to be pulled out of the closet for a few days at Christmas time, then forgotten and buried for the rest of the year. If we are to have peace and joy in our lives, it is to be remembered and lived every day of the year. By practicing unconditional love, we will be living the Golden Rule, and our lives will quickly change for the better.

Progress and Contemplation

Women/men are both spiritual and physical. We are the Universal Power in a physical body. As brothers and sisters, we are of this Essence, that is all one. The body is an individualization of it.

It is not always easy to love individuals when you look at them, but know they are more than their bodies, much more. The real spirit that each of us is, is part of the Spiritual Essence. It is this power within each of us that we can love and respect, even if the outside behavior seems lacking. Perhaps the purpose of life's journey is to make this discovery, for we are truly co-creators with this Energy. As a man thinks in his heart, so is he and his actions and creations. Furthermore, if ALL is created of the Universal Power, then Nature is part of It, and we need to harmonize with it.

I have indicated that just as languages serve a purpose of communication, so do religious teachings serve a purpose of communication. Love is the way, and knowing that is a great beginning, yet it is only a beginning. It is not just what we know that counts, but what we do with what we know. Are we truly practicing unconditional love in our everyday lives? If not, *why* not?

Part of the reason is our conditioning. We may fall short of the mark, but we don't have to stay there. We need to remember to be forgiving of ourselves too. When we can do that, it is usually easier to forgive others, for they too have made mistakes that they probably wish they hadn't made, and they too will be learning how to repair their errors. It is a learning process for all of us.

Part of this growing process is that we need to recognize our feelings and deep-seated beliefs, guilts, and frustrations, and work on them. They need to be healed and understood with love, too. So, be gentle with yourself.

All changes need to begin with *me.* How do we begin to love our brothers and sisters at the other end of the world, while at home we're still resenting a blood brother, fighting with our parents, judging our sisters, and upsetting other relatives, while complaining that the whole world is out of step?

It is, I feel, a matter of broadening our outlook, to use the Bible, the books on Buddhism, Confucianism, and other great truths and inspirational works, as a road map towards living a greater life, and *that* needs to be experienced.

For example: A singing instructor can tell me all about breathing, the theory of music, how to sing, and even demonstrate it, yet in the final analysis, if I am to sing, I have to experience it. Similarly, spirituality can be talked about, different approaches can be studied, and we may be guided by various sign posts, yet to understand it, one still needs to experience this for himself/herself. I'd like to share some exercises that may assist you in obtaining such an experience.

Relax the mind and body to the state that the mind becomes *uncluttered* from a *thousand things* running through it, and get to where you're thinking of *nothing*. At first this may seem difficult to do, but with practice, it becomes possible and effective, like the stilling of the ripples of a pond. You take time for work, play, and for meals, so invest a few minutes each day in this creative learning experience, to understand from deep within a knowing like one's conscience. This requires that for the moment you bypass your intellect and let your imagination or feelings take over. I therefore ask you to relax as though you were going to meditate, and in that relaxed state, contemplate on any one of the following ideas:

1) What is Love?
2) What is Nature, and how do I fit in with it?
3) Am I being true to me?

In this case, by contemplating, I mean just be aware of the sentence and see what comes bubbling up for you from within. Do *not* concentrate on it intellectually, but rather just allow your mind to drift while being aware of the sentence. Do not force or try to find an answer. Pretty soon ideas will start popping into your head, bringing with them feelings and, hopefully, new awareness.

Don't worry if at first you don't get any inspirational answers. Allow your mind to relax and observe whatever comes up for you. Don't make any judgments. Just *be* there. By practicing these types of exercises frequently, you'll start getting results. As you do, you will find yourself growing and becoming more interested and capable of being there for others, too.

Experiencing or "Feeling" Our Universal Power

Whatever your beliefs, recognize that the Universal Power is an artist constantly painting ever-changing sunrises and sunsets. It paints flowers with delicate fragrances. Take the time to smell them. It creates caterpillars that evolve into butterflies, and deserts, oceans, and birds, and all from Itself. It creates the animals and the forests, the mountains and the changing skies with sun, rain, lightning, and snow.

And let us not forget that It gives us a puppy and fills it with life, and It creates a mischievous, fun-filled kitten, too! And from the Magic of Itself, from Its very essence, It creates a baby. Each one of us *is* a baby of this Spiritual Nature, whatever our age. Think about that!

If we can view children as Its children rather than as ours, how much easier it would be for us to be considerate, respectful, understanding, and loving to them. As parents, we're the vehicles chosen to bring them into the world and to guide their development. What a privilege.

So we've established that we, each one of us, is a precious child of the Universe, made of the same Spiritual Essence. This thought is so awesome that we tend to block it out or reduce it to words and forget it. Do you believe that you are a part of the Universal Power? You can believe it, but will you?

What is true for you is also true of everybody else, and with the realization and acceptance that each of us is the Universal Spirit personified, it becomes easier to love, unconditionally. This Spiritual Essence that we are creates through us, and with the help of the natural resources that It has provided, we have learned to build our homes, offices, factories, and the stores that employ us. We've built automobiles for transportation and aircraft that give us a glimpse of the Universe.

Now there are spacecraft, the first vehicles to break our isolation on this planet earth, to propel us into the cosmos to explore the unknown as simultaneously we turn inward for the same reason.

Just as a few hundred years ago our ancestors discovered America, so, too, are we on a journey of discovery. What an exciting and spectacular era we are privileged to be living in, and how small and insignificant our problems when viewed from this larger perspective.

We have talked about an invisible something, The Universal Power, an intangible that is difficult for us to picture or grasp. With your permission and imagination, I would like to try to illustrate the concept. Imagine the Universal Power as the air that we breathe. We cannot see it, but we know that it is there. Now think of yourself as a limp balloon. It's pretty lifeless until the air fills it. Then the balloon becomes able to fulfill its purpose. You see, what we are is the Spiritual Power encased in our human bodies and the more aware we become of this Power, the more humane our actions are likely to be.

Being in these bodies, we are somewhat limited or restricted, and after a time of learning, it's time to become unrestricted again, so we let go of our bodies and become free again to blow in the winds and flow through the Universe. We're so much more than our bodies, though they are important in this lifetime, and, with the right attitude, exciting.

I now invite you to again think of a precious baby. Think of its little fingernails, its tiny hands and feet. Think of it cooing and think of its miniature heart beating with the Life Force, just like your heart and mine. It's truly the Essence of creation, with millions of cells, miles of veins, arteries, muscles, and bone.

How incredible this body is, and how fantastic this baby is as it begins to grow into childhood, getting into all the mischief that children will, going through the teenage stages, with all the learning that entails, and then into its adulthood, experiencing the pain of many errors as it grows from its mistakes.

Eventually, it becomes aware of forgiveness for its own growing mistakes, and for the growing mistakes of others. What a privilege to learn these lessons, even if it is often a hard or painful way to do it.

Finally we may grasp the beauty of spirituality and our oneness with it and one another, and desire to serve humanity.

Ultimately, our journey complete here, we let go of our bodies and return to the wholeness of our Spiritual Power and graduate to the next plateau of wisdom and even greater joy, experience, and wonderment.

Contemplate on this for a moment, and, as your Spiritual Self, experience the essence of your personal self, and the fact that we are really all Holy relatives. I love the Spiritual Power within you. I may not always agree with your actions, but I know that as you begin to recognize *your own divinity*, your actions will change appropriately towards loving unconditionally, which is living the Golden Rule; and isn't this truly what we *all* want?

The best way that I can help you grow is not to criticize and put you down, on the defensive or offensive, to prove myself right, but rather to love you by giving you space for self-discovery, and encouraging you in any way that I can.

Love has nothing to prove. It just IS.

I love you.

Just Thinking

How would it feel to live in a world of happiness, without wars, violence, famine, or abuse? The answer I'm seeking is, "Wonderful!" Was your answer perhaps, "What a dreamer; it'll never happen. He's crazy."

What if . . .

What if we had a magic wand that could bring about the changes we want. Would we use it? "Yes, of course!" you say. But remember the laws of nature—before you get heat from a fire, you have to put the wood in. Even with a magic wand, you'd still have to think what it is you want and don't want. Would you be prepared to "stop your world long enough to think about it?" Would you take the personal responsibility to use the magic wand?

The magic wand will give you the world of happiness that we talked about if you'll follow the instructions of how to use it. The instructions are very, very simple. There are only two instructions:

1) You must want, more than anything else, Peace, harmony, and happiness (which is what you say you want).

2) You must make a personal commitment to Love unconditionally (in order to attain it).

That means each of us must walk our talk, and that's what's been missing. We want these things, we talk these things, but it'll only happen with our *personal* commitment. Is asking *you* to *love* too high a price for you to live in Utopia? Will *you* use the magic wand or continue to live in the world just the way it is? You have the choice; you have the magic wand. Use it, or stop judging, complaining, and making the world worse, so that the rest of us can use our magic wands to create a world of Love, Peace, and Joy.

Perhaps now you're taking time out to think. (Good, it is one of the first ingredients of change.) Although we live in a wonderful world, we've created things that are unacceptable, such as wars, violence, and pollution. There are many reasons for this, including greed, selfishness, hate, revenge, and power, but there are some subtle, less recognized reasons, too, reasons that we may not want to look at or about which we want to remain in denial. To overcome problems, we need to put them out on the table for examination.

To help us create a Utopian world, religions have given us wonderful guidelines and insights, such as Living the Golden Rule, but the very religions that have brought us these wisdoms have also directly and indirectly brought about persecution, agony, and wars, both physical and psychological.

Religions' determination to be exclusive leads to differences. Differences can be healthy and, with new conflict resolution methods, lead to growth, but with *old thinking* they can be destructive, pitting Catholic and Protestant against each other, as in Ireland, and multiple-religions fighting, as in Bosnia, and until recently, in Lebanon. Even today, *Holy Wars* are still being waged.

Am I denouncing religion? The answer is both Yes and No, for I endorse the positive and constructive aspects, while deploring (rather than ignoring) the negative ones.

I was privileged to attend a meeting of "The Council for a Parliament of the World's Religions." According to the media, there were approximately 7,000 people at this conference. Gathered were religious leaders from all over the world. They were learned, educated, good, sincere people, all with one intent, to help bring Peace and harmony to the world, and I feel that they inspired us to do that. They stimulated people to go home and gather constructively together for the benefit of all. It was a privilege for me to meet these peoples with their hundreds of differing customs, life-styles, backgrounds, and beliefs. They were a reminder to me that we are all *People* sharing a rich diversity, just as our different nations share our one *Planet.* There was an obvious unity in the diversity as speaker after speaker spoke the wisdom of their religion, encouraging harmony and understanding. This conference was a milestone in my life, and I received many insights. I would like to share some of them with you.

I believe that just as America is a part of our planet, so is each person, individually and collectively a part of the Universal Spirit. We are all connected and interconnected.

Realizing that we are all just one people and one planet stimulated me to ask myself, What if there is *One* God and despite believing this, we created many Gods?

Until the conference, I believed in one God and that each religion chose to worship It in their own belief system, which tended to be exclusive rather than inclusive.

It was hard for me to accept that many in different religions would be so adamant that theirs was the right and only way, but then came an insight or understanding:

What if, instead of just being different religions, these different religions were worshiping different Gods? This had not occurred to me before, so I gave it a lot of thought and examination and found, as best I understand it:

Many Indigenous People worship The Great Spirit.

Jews worship the Lord their God.

Christians worship through Jesus, the Father.

Moslems worship through Muhammad, Allah.

Buddhists live by the Buddha nature.

The Bahá'í faith lives through Baha'u'llah, the common foundation of all religions.

Hindus contemplate Brahman or Atman, meaning God within.

And the list goes on.

For me, I now see that some people were not merely concerned with a religion, but concerned for their God. Let's build a rainbow which, like a transparent prism, reflects a multitude of colors. Not only does this rainbow encompass all of the colors, but it is also made up of all the religions and their Gods. If we were to call this rainbow the Ultimate Source, we'd see that we've just been arguing and fighting amongst ourselves unnecessarily. What a waste of joy, life, and energy. But we can remedy it so that everyone wins. What if the *Rainbow*, Universal Power, had lots of steps/ladders leading up to it?

As a prism includes all colors,

Yet is only one,

So too does The Great Spirit that is one,

Include all.

The Rainbow of Universal Power

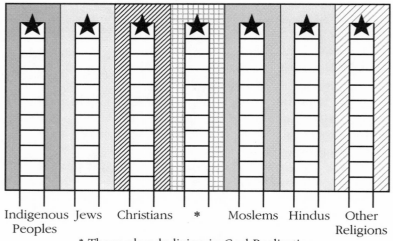

Indigenous Jews   Christians   *   Moslems   Hindus   Other
Peoples   Religions

* Those already living in God-Realization
because of different or personal experiences

Imagine Christians climbing their ladder, Jews climbing theirs, and Moslems and all the other religions approaching their own rainbow color. Think about that.

In each religion, people are at various stages of the ladder, some near the top, some in the middle, others near the bottom. We're all on the journey towards the Ultimate, whether we know it or not.

Some might approach the rainbow from having had a "life after death" experience.

Some may have touched this ecstasy through music, others may have experienced it through the miracle of birth, and still others have felt this while viewing a sunrise or a sunset, or while just smelling a rose.

The magnificent, brightly-colored rainbow is there for all of us (no more fighting), so choose your own ladder(s) of self-discovery, and climb. We may already be part of that rainbow, standing at each end *within* the pot of gold. Have we perhaps already found the pearl of great price? I believe that we have!

To me, we've been filling the glass with talk and watching it overflow and overflow. It's time to drink of the nectar, to savor the flavor, to drink in the perfume, and to *experience* that Spiritual ecstasy right here and now.

Consider how it might be if we were to retain our religious beliefs, yet move beyond the dogmas, and start trusting, believing, and accepting the miracle that *we already are,* part of the Universal Power's nature.

If we recognized and believed in our Spiritual perfection, we would not have to prove anything, we'd look just for the good in life, and that's what we'd find! Our ego characters would let go and accept our spiritual perfection, and our actions would begin to reflect this magnificent light within each of us.

Utopia is within our grasp; the Magic Wand is our Universal Power. It is our Spiritual perfection. Let's use It.

The Universal Power

The Universal Power contains *all* and is the essence of *all* religions, yet It is none of them. Some may describe it as heaven.

Everything is of Its manifestation, atoms, neutrons, and—most important for us to grasp and remember—we, individually, are a *personal creation* of this Universal Source/Essence. We search everywhere to find It, but that's *who we are* and *what we are*. We are designed to just *tune-in* to our Universal Power for guidance and direction. We receive our response through sudden inspirations, thoughts, flashes, or dreams that guide us with constructive options. Our intellectual minds receive these ideas from The Source, and we manifest them on this planet, with miraculous results.

The Universal Power *is* The Source of anything and everything that we can conceive of, and more, the seen and the unseen, and universes not yet seen or recognized. It's the timelessness that has always been, is now, and ever will be, and It's the *stillness* that remains constant while changing everything. It's the beauty beyond our greatest dreams or imagination and an unconditional love that we can hardly conceive of.

It's impossible to describe the Universal Power, for it's like the greatest paradox that isn't even a paradox, for the moment that you call It nothing, It's everything. It's unfathomable. It's like electricity. We do not see the *force*, yet we experience it and its results.

Air, too, is the Life Force (unseen, unless polluted), yet we cannot live without it. The Universal Source is that, too, and it's a constructive feeling, thought, hunch, or one's conscience. All of nature's creation is part of this sacred, ever-present Source. It's the all-knowing, all-encompassing Energy Force.

We sense and know Its presence, but the magnitude is so enormous that we feel we must continue to search for It through religions. Religions can and should be the guidelines of discovery that the Universal Power is what we are part of, and this realization would unify the people with each other, and with the Universal Spirit.

It's all here for us to enjoy right now. We need to believe, rejoice, and accept the magnitude of our beingness, our Spiritual selves.

A way to do this is to read inspirational books, then be still and reflect on their message. Such contemplation first thing in the morning will help start your day off right. Contemplation throughout the day will help you expand your awareness, and last thing at night your appreciation for it all will just add more to your blessings.

CLOSING

When a piece of sand enters an oyster, it creates a friction that causes the oyster constantly to excrete a membrane that covers the sand, and eventually it becomes a pearl.

If this book has in any way created discomfort, I hope that this irritation will lead you to seek the pearl of great price. I remind you that these views are my beliefs, and I hope that you share some of them. If not, it is my wish that this book may have encouraged you to search deeper into your own belief system, not so much with the words, but to seek deeply for the understanding of the Spirit of the word.

As you seek your destination, remember to enjoy your journey, walk your talk, be gentle with yourself and know that Peace begins with *you.*

I end this book as I began it, in awe, gratitude, and appreciation of the all-encompassing Great Spirit that I call God.

Attractive Traits to Seek

To bring more joy into your life, BE:

APPROACHABLE	FREE-THINKING
ALERT	FRIENDLY
ALIVE	GENEROUS
APPRECIATIVE	GENTLE
ASSERTIVE	GIVING
AWARE	GRACIOUS
CALM	HAPPY
CAPABLE	HEALTHY
CARING	HOPEFUL
CLEAN	HONEST
CONFIDENT	HUMBLE
CONFIDENTIAL	INDEPENDENT
CONFLICT-RESOLVING	INTERDEPENDENT
CONTENTED	INSPIRING
COOPERATIVE	INTERESTED
COMMUNICATIVE	INTERESTING
COURAGEOUS	JOYFUL
DEPENDABLE	KIND
DISCERNING	LEVEL-HEADED
EMPATHETIC	LIVING-IN-THE-NOW
ENCOURAGING	LOVING
ENCOMPASSING	LOYAL
ENERGETIC	NON-JUDGMENTAL
FLEXIBLE	SELF-IMPROVING

NON-MANIPULATIVE	SHARING
OPEN-MINDED	SPIRITUAL
OPTIMISTIC	STRAIGHTFORWARD
OUTGOING	STRONG
PEACEFUL	TIDY
POSITIVE	TRUSTING
RELAXED	TRUSTWORTHY
RELIABLE	TOLERANT
RESPONSIBLE	UNCLUTTERED
RESPONSIVE	UNBIASED
SELF-ACCEPTING	UNDERSTANDING
SELF-CONFIDENT	WELCOMING
SELF-CONTROLLED	WORTHY
SELF-ESTEEMED	YOUNG AT HEART

Contrast these ideals with the traits that pull us down, as in Appendix B. Recognize the importance of wise choices to attain the results that can bring you greater happiness, and be appreciative of your ability to direct your life towards a constructive, capable, and rewarding future.

All Problems
Stem From Fear

Here are some of the traits that keep us locked into unhappiness, through being:

ABUSIVE	DEPENDENT
AGGRESSIVE	DESPAIRING
ANGRY	DESPERATE
APATHETIC	DESPISING
ARROGANT	DESPONDENT
BETRAYING	DIRTY (lack of hygiene)
BLAMING OTHERS	DISHONEST
BORED	DISTRUSTING
BRUTAL	EGOCENTRIC
BULLYING	ENVIOUS
CLOSE MINDED	ESCAPING
CO-DEPENDENT	EXPECTANT
CONDEMNING	FALSE-BELIEVING
CONTROLLING	FRIGHTENED
CORRUPT	FRUSTRATED
CRITICAL	FURIOUS
CRUEL	GREEDY
DEFENSIVE	GUILTY
DEGRADING	HATEFUL
DEMANDING	HELPLESS
DENYING	HOPELESS

IGNORANT   SELFISH
INTOLERANT   SELF-LIMITING
IRRITABLE   SELF-REPROACHING
JEALOUS   SEPARATE
JUDGING   SHOULD-FUL (ordering)
LABELING   SICK
LACKING IN RESTRAINT   SPITEFUL
LAZY   SPOILING
LIVING IN THE PAST   STRESSED
LONELY   SULKING
LOW (SELF-ESTEEM)   TEMPERAMENTAL
LYING   (BAD OR HIGH) TEMPERED
MANIPULATIVE   UNAPPRECIATIVE
MISERABLE   UNAPPROACHABLE
MISERLY   UNCARING
NARROW-MINDED   UNCONTROLLED
NASTY   UNDEPENDABLE
NEGATIVE   UNFORGIVING
PESSIMISTIC   UNHAPPY
POUTING   UNLOVING
PREJUDICED   UNWORTHY
PRIDEFUL   UPSET
PUNISHING   VENGEFUL
RAGING   VICTIMIZED
REACTIONARY   VIOLENT
RESENTFUL   WEAK-WILLED
  (or burying it)   WICKED
RIGID   WORRYING

For Meetings and Conferences

May I humbly suggest that we commence any meeting by each, in our own way, taking a moment of silence or prayer, to evoke the blessings and wisdom of the Spiritual Power, that we may come to this event fully present, alert, peaceful, and relaxed, ready to give as well as to receive from one another. Let's take a minute of silence.

Thank you. May the spirit of love and compassion influence our every decision, making this meeting experience one of harmony, efficiency, and constructive action.

One Liners!

* Peace begins with Me.
* Live from peaceful action, rather than from angry reaction.
* Peace is not just the absence of war, but the presence of love.
* Peace is an attitude.
* Unconditional love is *Unconditional.*
* Thoughts manifest, so think constructively.
* Be still and know. Know the *stillness* that remains constant while changing everything.
* There is nothing to prove. Just Be!
* Don't hide your light, let it shine; you're wonderful.
* Love heals.
* Living the Golden Rule brings joy.
* Develop a win/win way of life.
* Look for the good in everything, especially in yourself.
* Be gentle with yourself; you are precious.
* Your Spiritual Power loves you, do you?
* I am no more and no less important than anyone else, and I'm more than just okay.
* I'm not my profession, nor am I my ego. I am a personalized, perfect child of the Universal Nature, just like you.
* The Essence of me is perfection waiting for my behavior to catch up.
* As we achieve a right relationship with the Universal Power, our relationship with the world and each other comes to life.

* Seek first the Kingdom of your Spiritual Essence, and all else will be added unto you—All, All, All else.
* The Spiritual Power is a perpetual discovery.
* Allow love to be your destination.
* To contemplate your Universal Power is like praying constantly.
* Meditation trains us to be calm, aware, and alert.
* To thine own self be true, first, foremost, and always, with consideration, love, and respect for others.
* Row, row, row your boat *gently* down the stream; go with the flow.
* Seek Unity in Diversity.
* Reading self-help books is good; applying their wisdom is better.
* It is not so much *what we know* that counts as much as *what we do* with what we know, and, paradoxically:
* Don't just do something, sit there!
* Life is a balance.
* This *AND* that offers more options than this *OR* that.
* We have freedom of choice.
* Freedom is not a license; it requires self-discipline and responsibility. It is a privilege.
* Nothing that we do in anger works constructively.
* If any motive is selfish or inconsiderate, reconsider it.
* Pride is a two-edged sword.
* Forgive yourself and others.
* It's in the giving that we receive.
* Preferences are pleasing; demands are disappointing.
* Problems are opportunities in disguise.
* Concentrate on what you stand for and for what you want, rather than wasting energy fighting what you don't want.
* What we resist, we encourage to persist.
* We are constantly receiving, transmitting, and projecting information from our own perspective.
* "Love the hell out of 'em!"

Dated Materials

Interdenominational Talk
August 1991

Dear People,

I appreciate, delight in, and give thanks for the work that's being done here to focus and increase the common denominators in our religious diversities, while at the same time respecting our differences. A wise Indian Chief was asked the question, "You smoke the peace pipe, but still there are wars. Why?" The Indian Chief pondered for a moment and replied, "Many people smoke the peace pipe, but few inhale." Friends, it's time that we inhale.

Jews are waiting for the Messiah to arrive, and Christians are waiting for Jesus to return. What kind of hosts are we? Is this world situation the incentive that we want to give Him? If I were He, I'd want to postpone my trip! One million nine hundred thousand U.S. dollars could feed thousands of starving children for years. But according to United Nations information, the world is currently spending that money, one million, nine hundred thousand U.S. dollars every hour of the day and night, approximately forty-eight million dollars per day, on the global military. Why? We're training our young people in the military to become barbaric, killing robots. Why? We continue to build military munitions of an incredible destructive capacity. Why? We are poisoning our air, water, and environment, clear-cutting our forests and killing off our animals.

Why? We're killing populations with contaminated wastes that we don't know what to do with. And even as it seeps into our soil, water, and oceans, we still continue to mine uranium and plutonium for military and civilian uses. Why? Why do we allow these appalling things to happen? Why? Why? Why? Why? Why?

We can no longer stand by and allow people to be rewarded for ignoring principles on account of greed, selfishness, and power. We all know that there are industrial groups, business conglomerates, and some unprincipled, power-hungry politicians who do not seem to care about the planet and its future. What we need to support and where we truly become useful as individuals and groups is in making the choice only to support those politicians and businesses that do care.

We who are gathered here must reach out to thousands of churches, temples, and mosques, to instruct them to influence their hundreds of thousands of congregations that we can allow no more killings, no more munitions, and no longer are we prepared to work for half a week to support our families and the other half to support government income taxes that are being squandered on the military, which is destroying us economically and socially. We can no longer encourage such world craziness. We have to change, we can change, and we must change. It is now that critical.

Without peace, everything is threatened. Your family, your home, your job, your possessions, and yes, your life. Our top priority has to become peace. Peace requires a massive, mature education, a self-examination, and an earnest desire to improve our individual peace efforts. *Peace begins with me as an individual. And just as other people's actions affect me, so also do my actions affect others.* We've literally become one interconnected body of humanity. *So how do I live on a day to day basis? Am I contributing joy and happiness towards a peaceful world, or aggravation and hostility for an aggressive one? I make a difference.* Each one of us makes a difference. Meanwhile, we can start with small things like a smile of encouragement, an encouraging word, and appreciation rather than criticism.

A child asked his father to play with him, and the dad gave him a jigsaw puzzle, saying, "You make that, and then I'll play with you." To his astonishment, the son came back fifteen minutes later with the puzzle completed. "How did you do that so quickly?" asked the father, "That was a map of the world." The child said, "On the other side was a picture of a man, and I knew that if I got the man right, the world would fall into place."

Our closed hearts contain an abundance of love, and everyone wants love. If I loved, I'd treat you as I'd like to be treated. So I ask, isn't that the kind of world that you'd like to live in? Perhaps as we let go of fear and open our hearts to loving and caring for each other, we will discover that the Messiah or Christ has arrived; not in the form of a person, but literally in the Spirit of love flowing from each of our hearts. What we are is children of that Universal Essence, blemished by worldly experiences, seeking our way home again. Open your hearts to one another. You're precious. Let your Inner Light shine brightly with unconditional love. That's all it takes for peace to come on the inside, and as a consequence, to the outside. Remember, *Peace begins with me. If not me, who and when?* I love you, *unconditionally.*

A Plea for Sanity / A Call for Action
October 1990

In the past there have been many wars, with troops giving their lives and limbs for the war to end all wars. I was deeply concerned that President Bush and Secretary of State Baker were preparing our allies for permission to start an offensive war. Each one of us is precious. We can no longer afford to risk even one life. We were not created to destroy one another. Now is the time that we should show our patriotism and loyalty by being courageous and strong enough to use our creativity and intelligence for peace, not stoop down to the level of dictators by ourselves becoming brutal and barbaric.

The imposed sanctions on Saddam Hussein are beginning to take effect. If we put as much effort into seeking a peaceful solution as we unfortunately do into a military one, we can succeed in having an armistice ahead of time, thus saving thousands of lives, limbs, and hardships that would otherwise be sacrificed. And for what? Would there be any oil left for anyone? And more important, would there be anyone left to use it? If we go to war this time, it could swiftly escalate throughout the world. No sane person could allow this to happen. We need to examine our values and ask ourselves, *What am I doing with my life? How do I spend my time?* Whatever our personal goals, we don't stand a chance if we blow ourselves up. There is nothing more important than peace. I feel that we can learn from the movie, *Born on the 4th of July.* It expresses great patriotism and depicts the futility and ineffectiveness of war. What is necessary is a massive, mature education of high principles, honesty, and human values. We can start here at home and let it expand outwards. This is a call for action. We can no longer afford apathy. We must get involved or perish. *Peace begins with me.* Each one of us makes a difference. For the sake of humanity, make yourself heard. Call or write your congressperson, or call the White House at (203) 456-1111. Please invite your friends, relatives, churches, businesses, and groups to join in. Do it now. Thank you, and may God's love run deep within your hearts.

Another Letter by Peace Pilgrim II November 1990

This is not a judgment, but rather a discernment, a call to what is. We are dealing with two power-hungry, egotistical people. One is Saddam Hussein, who is completely in charge of his country, unchallenged by it, and is used to having entirely his own way at any price. He would be prepared to die rather than lose face to his country and give in to world pressure to pull out of Kuwait. On the other hand, President Bush, carrying a big stick, is trying to bully

Hussein into pulling out of Kuwait, deflecting attention away from
our internal financial and other problems, gaining personal power in
1992, and for the glory of being a strong, tough President. He has
drawn a line in the sand, and seems unable to back down for fear of
being thought of as being weak or a coward, or of being questioned
as to how to justify sending all the troops, ships, and equipment at
the cost of who knows how many billions to our country, which is
already so hopelessly in debt. I hope that he is not thinking that the
only way for us to get our economy back is to go to war to
substantiate our building munitions, which is how Hitler built his
economy.

Surely President Bush must have some advisors who think
psychologically and can point out to him that Saddam Hussein, as a
dictator, will never be bullied into withdrawal. Hussein has continually, publicly pleaded for talks. It seems to me that we should listen
instead of being so obsessed with war. We already are, or are fast
becoming, the war mongers.

President Bush, please consider this possibility. You have
shown your courage, strength, and military commitment by amass-
ing an armada in Saudi Arabia; nobody doubts that you're wanting
to use it. Instead, why not call Saddam Hussein's bluff, go there with
a peaceful intent, and talk to him. This would be a win/win situation.
He can then save face with his country, because you, a world leader,
did as he requested and came to negotiate, and so he conceded to
withdraw, and that's what's important.

You, President Bush, would be a respected hero for, though
being poised for an attack, you took the initiative to talk Hussein into
giving you what you initially wanted, his getting out of Kuwait, all
this without a shot being fired and practically without the loss of life.
As a result, you would probably be reelected in 1992 and go down
in history as a strong President, wise enough to negotiate rather than
be responsible for the slaughter of hundreds of thousands and
maybe millions of people. I cannot believe that your conscience
would allow you to invite such mass murder while there are viable
options. Please, humble your ego to listen to your conscience.
Respectfully, Peace Pilgrim II.

Concerns and Solutions
September 10, 1986

Concerns

It is obvious that we are rapidly moving into a new era, one of utter and complete planet earth destruction or one of complete change from selfish, competitive survival and fear, to cooperation and mutual trust, understanding, and respectful concern for one another—as in love!

I will not dwell on the reasons that we may self-destruct; they're obvious. What is not so obvious is how to proceed with the alternative. It seems necessary, therefore, to point out the problems/ opportunities that we have to face in order to *sell* the people/ governments on wanting to *risk* making a change.

Here are the objections and concerns to overcome:

1) Fear: If we don't continue to arm, an enemy will arm, and we'll be defenseless when they attack. Therefore, continue to build arms until we all blow ourselves up.

2) Fear: Assuming that we stopped the arms race, immediately there'd be mass unemployment, bankruptcies, and monetary collapses. Everything would be in chaos.

This is probably a bigger underlying fear (for the greedy) than *putting off* world destruction as long as they can, by sweeping it under the rug. But we can no longer sweep it under the rug—we're too close to *pushing the button day* to dare to do that. We've got to make the choice. Change or die—that's the bottom line.

For some, to change seems scarier than to die unnecessarily. Maybe this is true for some, but we're not just talking about ourselves, we're talking about our children and grandchildren, too. Don't they deserve a chance to live, in a better world? We need to be looking at how to deal with the new opportunities caused through:

1) Mass unemployment (which we're going to have to do anyway, as computers and robots are already causing massive unemployment),

2) Bankruptcies and business failures, or

3) Monetary collapse (as bad or worse than 1929), which older people have experienced and fear. So, why would there be mass unemployment? And how would we deal with mass unemployment? Mass unemployment occurs as jobs become obsolete, for whatever reason. Right now, financial disaster is imminent as businesses/factories close. Seventy percent of business is engaged in the arms race, directly or indirectly. If this stops, you will see unemployment problems.

Solutions

Solutions have to be considered, and this requires us to go *out on a limb* for their discovery. We cannot look back in history for solutions (as lawyers do when they refer to old law cases for guidance). We are on the cutting edge of a new society; we have to let go of the old one, with its competition, heart attacks, questionable principles, alcoholism, drugs, and disease. The losing game, the treadmill of trying to *stay on top,* has to go.

The new society requires that our best brains and computers be put to work in facing the challenges, finding solutions, and implementing them. Let's examine some solutions and broadcast their possibilities so that we can open up some closed minds to see the benefits available—once people are shown attractive alternatives, they'll want them.

1) Let's switch from nerve gas and atomic bombs to "Big Sell" on benefits for "Not blowing ourselves up." Instead of money being spent on arms, spend it on radio and TV to show the benefits of cooperating with one another, programs of general benefit such as "Hands Across America"; start teaching in the schools how to live peacefully; and discourage toys of war, guns, tanks, battleships, and war planes. To start thinking globally, acting locally has already been verbalized; we need to bring it to life and to *do* it.

2) Let's start producing and employing only what we want for constructive and cooperative use. Repair the disastrous bridges about to collapse across our country. Create self-help programs, rail transit, education on alternative lifestyles—with an emphasis on exercise, health, prevention, nutrition, spare time, and joy in life. We

need massive help for alcoholics, addicts, prisoners, and the mentally disturbed, and aid for older people needing help and medical care. Let's encourage concern, understanding, and care alternatives for their loneliness and give encouragement for them to share of their experiences and be useful. Let's encourage them so that they don't feel that life's passed them by and that they're just taking up space waiting to die.

3) Finally, but most important, is to put our trust in the Universal Power, to exemplify the Essence of what all religions have tried to teach us, to *love one another.* That requires being honest with ourselves and others, cooperating in what's best for all of us; being free and wanting others to be free (not manipulative); and recognizing and encouraging our similarities and accepting our differences as being necessary for variety and freedom.

Courage
June 1991

This is a controversial article; do you have the courage to read it with an open mind? It's not just time for reflection, but more important, it's a time for projection. We in the U.S.A. are ecstatically waving our flags in the celebration of victory in the Gulf War. We are bringing our military personnel home as heroes for winning the war. Our country has rallied to support our troops, and they deserve that support because they did their job incredibly well. A superficial look at the benefits of the war show that:

1) We have won the war.

2) We have liberated Kuwait.

3) We have destroyed some of Iraq's military potential.

4) We have proved that our *smart* military equipment is effective, so again (good for our economy), we should continue to produce defensive armaments to replenish those used, and stockpile more. Based on the above successes, it seems that we'll continue more of the same.

Just perhaps there's another way of building the economy, one that does not take trillions and trillions of dollars to build human killing machines, and which, in order to be justified, will require us to create another war in twenty years time (and maybe that time, we'll be the ones pulverized).

It seems that in the brief six weeks of the war, our casualties were unbelievably light. We celebrate and thank the Universal Power for that miracle.

We mourn for the heroes who didn't make it home. Each person is very precious, and their loss is especially felt by their close relatives, their wives, husbands, and children, their brothers and their sisters, their parents and sweethearts, as well as their workmates and friends. How untimely and sad that their young lives of incredible potential had to be snuffed out because of war. Think about it, it might just as easily have been one of your loved ones mutilated for life or killed.

President Bush recently stated that he has nothing against the Iraqi people, it's just Sadam Hussein and his government that needed toppling. Shouldn't we then remember also to mourn for the tens of thousands of Iraqis and Kuwaitis who lost their lives and limbs to our *smart machines,* and for the agonies that their families are also going through?

The bottom line is that all people are unique, precious, talented, and doing the best they can. In some ways we've all been misdirected by giving up our power to leaders who skillfully brainwash us into their belief systems of creating enemies and justifying our actions. We call ourselves civilized, but are we? Isn't the time long overdue for us to wake up and realize that we were created to love one another? Isn't love what we really want—to understand and be understood, to be respected and cared for as a human being? We have the potential and ability to create a Utopia, and love is what it takes. We must no longer allow ourselves to slaughter one another through misunderstanding, power, greed, pride, ambition, or for any other reason.

We must demand through the U.N. that:

1) All countries in the world cease to produce any more killing machines, and dismantle those remaining.

2) A Peace Force of the United Nations be the ONLY force to have minimum military for any disturbances across the globe.

3) Militaries in all countries convert to take care of natural disasters and constructive projects such as rebuilding failing bridges throughout the country. Presently they play brilliant war games which in reality become barbaric and are archaic.

For so long it's sounded like a trite saying, but honestly, isn't it time to *give peace a chance?* Each country should establish a peace office. Fortunes that are currently wasted on munitions could cut down the crime of enormous income taxes, which we the people are paying for this craziness. We should be encouraged to become humanized again, caring for one another and seeking the best for each other. If we're to survive as a species, we've got to work together on enormous global projects such as ecology and changing our educational priorities towards how to learn to live with each other.

At the top of the list of humanities subjects should be:

1) Conflict resolution, or how to talk out our differences instead of using brute force.

2) Parenting, as many of us come from dysfunctional homes, and we urgently require new guidelines. People who treat their children poorly aren't usually *bad* people, but frustrated by not knowing how to care properly.

3) Response-ability, or being able to respond from a loving heart instead of reacting in anger. Also, boys need to be taught of their financial and other responsibilities, should they get a girl pregnant, so that they'll think twice before treating sex as a game or status symbol, and we'll have fewer abortion concerns.

4) Health and appreciation, or how to take care of our magnificent bodies rather than abusing them.

5) We need to teach high principles—honesty and human values, self-esteem, consideration, a *giving* rather than a getting attitude, and a healthy discernment rather than guilt producing judgment. What is required is an appreciation for everything,

especially life. These are some constructive, preventive *how-tos,* which may take time to learn, but which are more effective rather than relying on band-aids like extra prisons or drug and alcohol rehab centers that can only help *after the fact.*

Wishing You Bountiful Life's blessings,

Love, Peace Pilgrim II

To arrange for talks or workshops,
please call or write,
Peace Pilgrim II
c/o Blue Dolphin Publishing, Inc.
P.O. Box 1920 • Nevada City, CA 95959
(916) 265-6925 • FAX (916) 265-0787

Peace in back of handcart

Peace cane to Port Orford last week ... pushing a two-wheeled blue handcart that held a duffle bag containing all his worldly possessions: a few clothing items, some toilet articles and a smidgen of dried fruit to sustain hi____ en times get tough____ g stretch b____

____ce Pil-
____ on October 2, to ____ word of peace among ____ool students, church congregations and people he meets during his travels.

Peace Pilgrim II keeps spreading love message

____ behind ____
cl____ life in Eu____
with a home and ____
that goes with i____
mits to being in ____
answered a "ca____
and ____ding the w____
pea____ ____ths ago
hea____
an____
w____
a____
th____
a____

____myself a millionaire.
____nt attitude and ____ou happy ____nt

Rules of the road hard for Peace Pilgrim II

He's home, the traveler with tales from the road, with some ailments that threaten his mission, but with a commitment to continue.

he did jus____ ____t
talked to students and Driftwood elementary on Tuesday spoke to Pacific high school, and ussed to the high school ___co junior high in Lang-

He's walking for peace

by Dirk Vinlove

A march for peace continues thanks to a man's inner calling that required discarding all worldly possessions and hitting the road for the rest of his life.

except the clo____
cart, duffle and what's in it. D____

____was to resume his journey